SMART TENNIS

SMART TENNIS

How to Play and Win the Mental Game

John F. Murray, Ph.D.
Rick Frey, General Editor

JOSSEY-BASS
A Wiley Company
www.josseybass.com

Published by

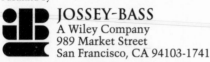

JOSSEY-BASS
A Wiley Company
989 Market Street
San Francisco, CA 94103-1741

www.josseybass.com

Credits are on p. 237.

We at Jossey-Bass strive to use the most environmentally sensitive paper stocks available to us. Our publications are printed on acid-free recycled stock whenever possible, and our paper always meets or exceeds minimum GPO and EPA requirements.

Library of Congress Cataloging-in-Publication Data

Murray, John F.
Smart tennis : how to play and win the mental game /
John F. Murray ; Rick Frey, general editor. — 1st ed.
p. cm. — (Smart sport series)
Includes bibliographical references and index.
ISBN 0–7879–4380–0 (cloth : acid-free paper)
1. Tennis—Psychological aspects. I. Frey, Rick. II. Title.
III. Series.
GV1002.9.P75 M88 1998
796.342'2—dc21 98–40156

PB Printing 10 9 8 FIRST EDITION

To my wife, Charlotte,
to my mother and father,
and to both our families
—J.F.M.

Contents

Smart Sport Series Preface

Have you ever imagined performing your favorite sport without error, as effortlessly as the sport's greatest athletes?

Have you ever had a feeling of absolute self-confidence just before performing?

Have you ever set short-, medium-, and long-range goals relative to your sport performance . . . and fully expected to reach one?

Did you ever have so much fun participating that you never wanted to stop?

Twenty-five years ago, most recreational, college, and even national-level athletes would have answered no to such questions. In fact, back in the 1970s when questions like these were first being asked by sport psychologists around the country, athletes and their coaches often only shook their heads over them, amused that anyone would ask.

Things have changed over the last quarter-century. Today, when such questions are asked of the full range of sport participants—from beginning athletes to world-class champions—the answers are usually yes.

Yes, I can imagine error-free, effortless performance.

Yes, I've felt total self-confidence prior to sport performance.

Yes, I've set, and expected to achieve, my personal sport performance goals.

Yes, I've really experienced a great deal of enjoyment while participating in my sport.

It seems that most of us who are involved in sport, and even a good share of nonparticipants, know about—and have attempted—various performance enhancement techniques that involve psychology. Knowledgeable sport coaches and sport psychologists refer to these techniques as psychological skills training—or simply as mental training. But not everyone who can answer yes to these and other mental training questions necessarily reaches full potential in sport, gets the most enjoyment from sport, or even continues to rehearse and refine his or her mental training techniques. Why not?

The main reason is that most individuals below the elite level of competition do not practice their mental skills with the same consistency that they devote to their physical training. This results, unfortunately, in a great number of sport participants who know about mental training but are not sure how to go about it effectively nor how to use it to improve their physical skills and enjoyment. Thus their answers to the questions might be extended as follows:

I can imagine error-free, effortless performance—but I just can't seem to make the images translate to my physical performance.

I've felt total self-confidence prior to sport performance, only to find my self-assurance disappear as soon as I started participating.

I've set, and expected to achieve, my personal sport performance goals—but after a few successes, I've been unable to reach the others.

I've really experienced a great deal of enjoyment in my sport, but when I feel like I'm not improving, the fun wears off.

The book you hold in your hands is one in a series published by Jossey-Bass designed to bring sport-specific applied sport psychology to a new level of sport participant trustworthiness and practicality. To begin with, the books in the Smart Sport Series are written by experts not only in the specific sport under discussion but also in applied sport psychology. Each of the books in the Smart Sport Series has a common backbone of content to ensure that the most important and widely applicable elements of sport psychology are treated in each of the titles in the series. Each covers the principles and practical aspects of achievement motivation, arousal regulation, psychological skills training, self-confidence, goal setting, concentration, and enjoyment pertinent to the sport under discussion. Other features:

- Self-tests help you evaluate your current status in a variety of sport psychology and mental skills areas.
- Special highlight boxes make it easy to comprehend and remember key points.
- Focused bibliographies help you find the most significant references on important topics.

Finally, each of the series books is rich in examples to help you understand and internalize the principles that can lead you to a higher level of sport performance. This combination of expert writing, sport expertise, core psychological principles, and sport-specific examples helps make the Smart Sport Series the smart choice for both male and female athletes of all ages and abilities who are looking to move to the next level of personal achievement.

Each book in the Smart Sport Series is a tool. For beginning athletes, it can serve as an enlightening introduction to a new sport. For veterans, it can assist in the repair of faulty performance and improve an already solid technique and strategy. For everyone, it can help build a new model of sport-specific learning and personal understanding that can take you closer to your personal best.

I encourage you to use this book to help find that peace of mind that comes from knowing you've done your best in sport to become the best you are capable of becoming!

RICK FREY, PH.D.
GENERAL EDITOR

Preface

Welcome to an exciting personal journey. Whether you play or coach tennis professionally, slug it out on the weekends, or just want to develop the mental skills of a champion, *Smart Tennis* is your comprehensive user's guide and companion. This book will lead you toward self-understanding, improvement, and greater enjoyment in tennis.

Although many agree that tennis is at least 75 percent mental, they often neglect the mental game—limiting their success and enjoyment. You have in your hands the most useful information on the mental aspects of tennis. Even more useful than a set of tips on scouting the players in your next tournament, *Smart Tennis* helps you identify your own strengths and weaknesses to help you win the game against your toughest opponent—yourself! Place it in your racket bag, keep it near the bed, or lend it to your doubles partner, but don't share it too soon with your favorite opponent!

This book applies to players at all levels from beginners to world champions. These principles and tips really work. I've helped both elite and recreational athletes use them, and they'll work for you. Use them not only in tennis but in many other competitive endeavors. Although the context is tennis, these tools of sport psychology can be used far and wide.

I've played and coached tennis all over the world with players at every level from barefoot novices on the steaming asphalt courts of Saudi Arabia to ranked professionals on the green clay of Florida. I've taught tennis to world leaders at resorts in Europe and Hawaii, and introduced the game to tribal natives in Thailand. Regardless of age, culture, ATP ranking, or position in life, one thing is always clear—tennis inspires everyone.

I've enjoyed sharing my knowledge by publishing over seventy articles on tennis and sport psychology, promoting tennis via radio, and keeping up with readers of my regular sport psychology column. I've also enjoyed conducting sport psychology seminars at the ATP Tour International Headquarters and working closely with many collegiate tennis players. My experience in sport psychology extends to many other sports as well. For example, I conducted my doctoral dissertation on the national champion Florida Gators football team, and served one year as sport psychology intern at Washington State University.

As a tennis player and coach, I was often dismayed by the lack of high-quality materials on the mental aspects of the game. While training to become a clinical psychologist and sport psychologist I was even more annoyed! Why were so few resources available? First of all, sport psychology is still a young discipline, and scientific findings take time to reach interested players. Second, there are very few qualified sport psychologists with an understanding and love of tennis to communicate this knowledge. Finally, available materials on tennis psychology are written by authors of varying backgrounds. To my knowledge this is the first written by an author combining expertise in tennis, sport psychology, and clinical psychology. This book shares my enthusiasm in all three disciplines.

Smart Tennis helps you understand tennis and the psychology of performance as never before. You have the latest and most accurate word on tennis psychology presented in a clear and concise manner.

Although sport psychology is fast becoming one of the best means of enhancing performance, no message is any good if not heard. With this in mind, Chapter One is designed for you to get to know your whole self better. Like a sport psychologist, this chapter helps you understand your own game. In fifteen to twenty minutes, you rate yourself on a hundred psychological insights important in tennis. The self-scoring system identifies your strengths and weaknesses and classifies you into one of twenty possible Need Types. You're then given specific direction for rapid and meaningful improvement! You become a better and much more satisfied player as your game evolves.

Specific techniques are presented in subsequent chapters to help you eliminate the many distractions that interfere with success and enjoyment. These may be thoughts and feelings such as anger and fear, or external conditions like rude opponents and weather.

Because you can never achieve your peak performance while distracted, Chapter Two introduces attention control as a crucial foundation in enhancing your game. How well you maintain focus often spells the difference between optimal performance and mediocrity. There's nothing more exhilarating than being in the "zone" with complete attention and effortless play. More about the zone later!

A wide variety of mental and physical skills are enhanced by imagery, which is introduced in Chapter Three. Imagery (or visualization) is your brain's computer software—it programs your thoughts and feelings, providing you a virtual reality of events before they occur. When imagery is used properly, you win the battle with yourself by managing your thoughts, feelings, and behavior more effectively. The latest techniques in tennis imagery are presented in a user-friendly manner.

Chapter Four helps you develop and maintain confidence, that incredibly powerful awareness that you will perform your absolute best. If overconfidence or underconfidence is ever a problem, this chapter will straighten you out. Confidence is attainable by all, regardless of ability, and confident players always perform better.

In Chapter Five you're provided with the solution to energy management. If overexcitement, anxiety, or reduced energy levels have ever impaired your play, this chapter will help you create an optimal energy mixture for success.

Goal setting, a remarkably effective motivational tool, is discussed in Chapter Six. Players setting inappropriate goals—or no goals—always fail to reach their potential. With goal setting in hand, you'll have unlocked the door to top performance and fulfillment.

Chapter Seven integrates all these fundamental skills into your actual pre-tournament and match day activities. You'll see how to apply hands-on mind-body techniques before, during, and after a competition with plenty of examples. Smart tennis players use this chapter to make performance efficient and exciting.

When you are better acquainted with your whole person and have applied the principles of smart tennis to your advantage, you'll view tennis, sport, and performance in a totally new way. With this latest scientific expertise and practical wisdom, you'll be much more relaxed before important matches, worry less about losing, and greatly reduce choking. You'll gauge your performance by new standards, focusing on important mind-body tools rather than on outcomes.

The ultimate benefit of *Smart Tennis* is better self-understanding and an individualized plan to maximize your potential in tennis. It's my hope that you'll be stimulated and challenged along the way. Good reading and good tennis!

North Palm Beach, Florida JOHN F. MURRAY
December 1998

Acknowledgments

This book is the culmination of years of enlightening experiences in tennis, the sport sciences, and clinical psychology. I owe a tremendous debt of gratitude to the many tennis players and coaches I've worked with worldwide, to my friends and colleagues at the University of Florida and Washington State University, and to the students and clients with whom I've been fortunate to collaborate. I thank John Bowen for showing me how to make tennis a way of life. His wisdom and enthusiasm as a tennis champion, coach, and friend made it all easy. I thank Cliff Kurtzman for the opportunity to speak with the online tennis community in my monthly sport psychology column, "Mental Equipment," on the Tennis Server (http://www.tennisserver.com). I'm extremely grateful to Rick Frey, the Smart Sport Series general editor, for encouraging me to write this book—his knowledge, guidance, and support were invaluable. I also acknowledge the wise counsel of Alan Rinzler, my editor from Jossey-Bass, whose insights into the manuscript were crystal clear. Finally, I extend a special appreciation to my wife, Charlotte, and to all my family and friends who make it all worthwhile.

SMART TENNIS

1

Understanding Your Personal Needs

Jack Patterson, a commercial real estate agent in his late twenties, had a real drive to excel. Introduced to tennis by one of his clients, he knew right away that he wanted to become the best player he possibly could. He took lessons on technique and read everything he could get his hands on about the sport. After four years, however, he felt as if he'd come about as close to his personal potential in tennis as he could get. Although he could hold his own against many of the individuals he played regularly with, he was starting to feel unchallenged by the sport. He knew he wasn't the player he had once believed he could be, but he didn't know how he could get any better. That's when he met Marcia Alexander, a sport psychologist with a background as a tennis teaching professional.

After hitting with Marcia one afternoon, she asked him a question that eventually changed his approach to tennis—and his life outside the sport as well. Her simple question was: "Jack, what do you really know about yourself?"

Three months later Jack was a different person both on and off the tennis court. Using a simple paper-and-pencil test that Marcia provided, Jack got some insight into his personal strengths and weaknesses. Jack discovered that some of the things he knew about himself but had never really examined before were verified by Marcia's assessment. He also discovered that there were some areas in his life that he'd never known about himself; but upon reflection, he realized that they were accurate. For example, Jack scored low on one subscale that measured general confidence. When he saw that score and listened to Marcia's interpretation, he thought there must be some mistake. He was one of the most confident people he knew. He was bright, energetic, and had a good career. Why shouldn't he feel confident?

After some reflection, Jack took a better look at himself and realized that most of the time it wasn't feelings and thoughts of future success that drove him forward in his work, in tennis, and in life generally—it was feelings and thoughts of avoiding failure. "Just don't lose!" was his usual battle cry before a match. And that's the way he played: overheads that he could smash easily were hit with low power to push them into a safe place on his opponent's side of the net, second serves were practically hit sidearm to guide them carefully into the service court, and a defensive lob was his usual answer to an opponent rushing the net. Jack had wondered why he played so much more freely—with so much more flow—when he had a big lead, or even when he felt hopelessly behind in a match. As Marcia helped him see, in those cases the outcome of the match was pretty much decided. He had nothing to lose!

Jack marveled at his newfound insight. With Marcia's help, he began experimenting with ways to create positive feelings of confidence and flow from a variety of earlier experiences. Combined with his awareness of some other strengths and weaknesses, Jack was able to accentuate the positive, eliminate the negative, and slowly become a better tennis player. Much to his amazement, he also found that there was some transfer from the court to his career and life in general. He began to look at difficult situations as opportunities and to concentrate on approaching success instead of avoiding failure. By getting to know himself better, Jack identified areas where he could make changes in the way he perceived stress. Learning about himself was the first step Jack took to become a better player . . . and a better person.

Tennis helped Jack grow in many areas of his life. What excites you the most about tennis? Is it competing, staying fit, or just challenging yourself to become your very best? Whatever your interest, you are definitely not alone. Tennis is a passion for millions all over the world. Whether you play for a living or merely live for the chance to play, you owe it to yourself to become the best and smartest tennis player imaginable. The challenges of tennis for the beginner are just as thrilling as those for the world-class champion.

> Tennis is the most beautiful sport there is. It is also the most demanding. It requires body control, hand-eye coordination, quickness, flat-out speed, endurance, and that strange mix of caution and abandon we call courage. It also requires smarts. Just one single shot in one exchange in one point of a high-level match is a nightmare of mechanical variables.
>
> —David Foster Wallace

The benefits of tennis are endless. It only takes an hour to achieve a body-wrenching workout and total release from stress. It stretches your intellectual capacity and imagination while strengthening your bones and muscles. It is also a very social sport and can be started at almost any age and played forever. You can even challenge the opposite sex and easily find your match! Have you chosen tennis for any of these reasons?

In tennis you can always improve. Although there are a thousand different levels of play, Pete Sampras and Jane Doe can both experience the same enjoyment, health, and mental challenge when they play. What are your goals? Whether you hope to learn tennis, earn a college scholarship, or just capture Wimbledon, you have definitely chosen a winning sport.

The approach outlined in *Smart Tennis* is easy to understand and guaranteed to improve your game. It combines the latest tools of sport psychology and tennis expertise to sharpen your mental skills to the highest level possible.

Later in this first chapter you'll identify your own psychological strengths and weaknesses in tennis by completing the Tennis Mind-Body Checklist (TMBC), which I have used in my work with tennis players. The vast majority of tennis and sport psychology books provide advice without finding out who you are first. If you first get to know yourself better, the techniques and advice in this book will make more sense and apply more directly to your individual needs. If, on the other hand, you have little interest now in self-understanding, just skip ahead to Chapter Two and return to Chapter One at a later date.

The most popular personality questionnaire has 567 items and takes over an hour to complete! Don't worry, the TMBC has only a hundred true/false items and takes only fifteen to twenty minutes. It is very easy to score and interpret, and personal instructions are given on how to improve fastest. The short period of time it takes to complete the TMBC is worth more than years of training without self-awareness!

Whole-Person Approach

What you see is not what you get in tennis. Though exciting to watch, skilled play involves much more than perfect strokes, agility, and power. These physical factors, though important, only tell a partial story. Perceptions, thoughts, feelings, and tactics are just as essential. Many neglect mental skills, forfeiting a major advantage. In a whole-person sport, neither mind nor body must be forgotten.

I'm always horrified watching tennis instructors who stand in one position with a large basket of balls and reel off monotonous phrases such as "watch the ball," "bend your knees," and "racket back." A boom box attached to a ball machine would produce the same effect! Finding high-quality instruction can be challenging, but high-quality mental training is even rarer. This doesn't change the fact that mental skills are essential. The immortal Jimmy Connors recognized the importance of the whole-person perspective when he claimed that more than 95 percent of tennis at the pro level is mental. At any level of play, mental skills are extremely important. Many now believe this, but only a few train their psychological skills effectively. Those making the greatest strides, however, invest in mental as well as physical training. *Smart Tennis* will give you the mind-body advantage for the twenty-first century.

Do you ever have trouble advancing to a higher level in tennis? Is there one player you just can't seem to beat despite many near misses? Sport psychology has advanced in recent years to provide solutions to many of these problems. The strategies described in *Smart Tennis* were derived over years of research and experience in the sport sciences, psychology, and tennis. If you are a recreational player with little time to sift through endless studies and statistics, this is your sourcebook. If you're a professional looking for an extra edge, this is your best friend.

In times of difficulty, *Smart Tennis* also offers clues to get you back on track. Optimal performance for the smart tennis player is just an extension of a newly developed whole self. Careful attention to both mental and physical skills is needed for developing a whole game.

Since tennis is so wonderfully complex, it is an ideal means of testing mind-body skills to the limit. But tennis is just one area of performance. The principles and skills needed in this sport apply well in many other performance situations. For example, if you want to improve your public speaking, academic performance, or business productivity, smart tennis principles are a valuable asset.

You Start with ACES

ACES is the acronym I developed to represent four ways in which mind-body skills are expressed in tennis and in other performance situations too: *A*ctions, *C*ognitions, *E*motions, and physical *S*ensations. Although all four dimensions are represented in all tennis players, your path to greater tennis success likely differs from that of your neighbor. Your personal ACES profile sets you on the path you need most, given your current game.

Nothing can be loved or hated unless it is first known.
—Leonardo da Vinci

While certain players benefit most by concentrating on actions, others should place greater emphasis on cognitions or thoughts. Still others should emphasize emotions or feelings, while a fourth group should attend more to physical sensations. ACES helps you identify the means of expression needing most improvement at any given time.

In addition to ACES, your self-discovery involves determining which mind-body skills need the most development. The five skill areas include attention control, imagery, confidence, energy management, and goal setting. *Smart Tennis* presents each skill in a separate chapter.

When you have completed and scored the TMBC

you will know which chapters to focus on to really improve your game. Your responses to the TMBC also place you into one of twenty separate Need Types according to your scores on ACES and the mind-body skills. Finding your current Need Type is an exciting discovery and provides you with explicit instructions on becoming a smart tennis player.

For example, those with an A-A Need Type (Actions and Attention) will want to focus diligently on actions and behaviors that improve concentration, while those with an E-E Need Type (Emotions and Energy) will be better served by learning how their emotions affect their energy levels in tennis.

Sport psychologists consult with many of today's top tennis players, athletes from other sports, and even corporate athletes looking for a competitive edge. The most effective ones get to know their clients' strengths and weaknesses before making any recommendations. Whether you hire a sport psychologist or apply this book, ongoing self-discovery is required to gain direction and perspective needed for lasting improvement. *Smart Tennis* makes developing self-knowledge easy—all you need to do is complete and score the Tennis Mind Body Checklist (TMBC)! Before you go any further, find a time and place where you will be undisturbed for fifteen or twenty minutes and settle down with the questions in the checklist.

Tennis Mind-Body Checklist

The Tennis Mind-Body Checklist (TMBC) is designed to help you understand yourself better. Have you found a quiet place where you will be undisturbed? OK, let's get started.

Instructions

Read each question and answer true or false by placing a T or F in the blank provided. If you are not sure about a particular response, or it just doesn't seem to apply, answer in a way that most closely approximates your view, or how you think you would respond if it did apply. No single answer matters that much! Scoring and interpretation are easy, but you need a full set of answers. You'll find straightforward guidelines to help you apply the results later in Chapter One. Have fun!

Answer T (True) or F (False) to every question:

1. ______ My feelings usually help me maintain focus on the game.
2. ______ I monitor and adjust my bodily sensations to remain confident during a match.
3. ______ Goals that can be measured (such as first serve percentage) are more useful than those not easily measured (such as improved footwork).
4. ______ I've not learned to synchronize my breathing patterns with my tennis strokes.

5. _____ Only one sense at a time should be involved when using imagery.
6. _____ I imagine myself in many situations before, during, and after a tennis match.
7. _____ I often lose my concentration or focus because of internal sensations.
8. _____ I place most of my energy on winning matches rather than attempting to perform my best.
9. _____ I re-create positive, confident feelings in preparation for an upcoming match.
10. _____ I often feel so emotionally drained before a match that it is hard to keep my energy up throughout the match.
11. _____ I draw from an internal source of physical energy to play important points to the best of my ability.
12. _____ Practicing an imagination technique once a week is sufficient for a player who plays tennis three times a week.
13. _____ Relaxing thoughts seldom occur to me in between points.
14. _____ Others would say that I stay "in the moment" when I play.
15. _____ I very rarely play tennis against those below my ability level.
16. _____ The key in setting tennis goals is to set your sights as high as you possibly can.
17. _____ My breathing patterns fluctuate so much throughout a match that my game is thrown off.

18. _____ I make self-statements to fire myself up or calm myself down during competition.
19. _____ Prior to serving, I often visualize myself hitting an ace.
20. _____ Goals that instruct you to "do your best" are better than goals with specific aims (such as hitting more first serves in).
21. _____ Internal physical sensations change frequently, making it hard to concentrate.
22. _____ I don't really believe in my ability to achieve my objectives in tennis.
23. _____ My emotions change frequently in a match, throwing off my focus.
24. _____ My confidence is reduced because I experience physical tension in a match.
25. _____ It's not important to restrict myself by placing a deadline date for goal completion.
26. _____ No matter what the situation is, I'm able to keep from being over- or underenergized.
27. _____ I rarely get myself in a relaxed and focused state and imagine myself playing good tennis.
28. _____ I have a consistent routine (or ritual) that I always use to maintain focus.
29. _____ Visualization (or imagery) techniques are better for practicing physical skills than for practicing mental states.
30. _____ I often fail to get enough rest before matches and as a result find it hard to compete.

31. ______ In a very close match, I'm able to control my thoughts and energy level.
32. ______ During a rally, I often think of things unrelated to tennis, impairing my concentration.
33. ______ I often recite things to myself to improve my confidence during a match.
34. ______ I usually feel confident in anticipation of the start of a match.
35. ______ I play tennis more to demonstrate that I'm better than my opponent than to improve my own skill level.
36. ______ I view nervousness in tennis negatively.
37. ______ Having a solid knowledge of strokes and strategy is important to get the most out of imagination exercises.
38. ______ When using imagery in tennis, it's usually best to use an external perspective, as if I were a spectator watching myself play.
39. ______ I often watch successful tennis players to build up my own confidence.
40. ______ I set tennis goals that lead to steady progression toward improvement.
41. ______ I experience positive emotions that fire me up on the most important points.
42. ______ Those who watch me play would say that I usually appear quite focused on the match.
43. ______ When I'm behind in a match, I often experience positive feelings about my ability to come back.

44. ______ In the heat of competition, I experience physical sensations of positive excitement.

45. ______ Reevaluating goals regularly helps keep my motivation high.

46. ______ I never daydream in detail about how I will play various points of a match.

47. ______ My physical sensations usually remain stable because I'm focused on the present.

48. ______ Setting a goal to "win the match" is usually less helpful than a goal to perform better.

49. ______ Whether a goal can be measured or not matters little in selecting a goal.

50. ______ I often experience physical symptoms of anxiety (such as increased pulse rate or sweating) that disrupts my play.

51. ______ When I imagine myself playing tennis, it's usually as though I am actually playing rather than viewing myself from the outside.

52. ______ In the midst of a long rally, negative feelings seldom occur to me.

53. ______ I'm often physically nervous, lowering my confidence.

54. ______ Others know when I'm losing by just watching my body language.

55. ______ I often feel worried in pressure situations and cannot perform well.

56. ______ Looking at a photo in a tennis magazine is a good way to enhance mental rehearsal techniques.

57. _____ I often imagine myself becoming more confident and relaxed in pressure situations.

58. _____ When an opponent starts to rally and come back against me, I often let fear destroy my confidence.

59. _____ I often appear tense between points and lose focus.

60. _____ I do not reevaluate my goals in tennis because it's better to keep goals firm once they have been set.

61. _____ I often play out points in practice, making these points as realistic as possible to simulate match play.

62. _____ Once I've learned to use imagery properly, I should still practice it regularly to derive maximum benefit.

63. _____ I sometimes change my thoughts to remain focused on the game.

64. _____ There's no need to set goals for steady progression in tennis.

65. _____ Internal sensations often lower my confidence in my abilities.

66. _____ I set easy goals that can usually be reached rather than difficult goals that require strong effort.

67. _____ During changeovers, I focus awareness on my energy level and fire myself up or calm myself down as needed.

68. ______ Prior to a match, I find a relaxing and quiet place where I focus on performing my shots.
69. ______ Seeing myself play out points in my mind during changeovers is not a good idea.
70. ______ I usually have positive thoughts between points.
71. ______ When I have negative thoughts during a match, I immediately replace them with more positive ones.
72. ______ I set goals for each practice session.
73. ______ It's better to set specific goals (such as "win four games") than general goals (such as "do my best").
74. ______ Thoughts that I'll lose the match often make it hard to keep my stamina up.
75. ______ Watching tennis on television is not a good idea before using an imagination strategy.
76. ______ I use imagery to simulate the physical sensations that I actually experience while playing tennis.
77. ______ Frequently seeing myself lose a few points is helpful in using imagery, because it creates a more realistic scene in my mind.
78. ______ My feelings often change because I focus on past mistakes.
79. ______ Improving my level of play is more important than showing superiority.

80. _____ Knowledge of stroke production is of no real advantage in using mental rehearsal techniques.
81. _____ I set realistic goals rather than shoot for the stars with goals that have little chance for success.
82. _____ I tend to lose my confidence because of poor play.
83. _____ Relaxed muscles allow me to keep my cool during play.
84. _____ When I perceive my opponent to have superior talent, I rarely maintain feelings of confidence in my own ability.
85. _____ In setting a goal for tennis, I set a target date for completion rather than leaving that date open.
86. _____ Setting goals for practice is not really that important, as the focus should be more on achieving relaxed play.
87. _____ I love playing tennis, especially when the score is close in the final set.
88. _____ I'm able to block out fatigue to keep my energy level up during the late stages of a match.
89. _____ Daydreaming about playing tennis should involve as many different senses as possible.
90. _____ My focus is often ruined by negative internal feelings.

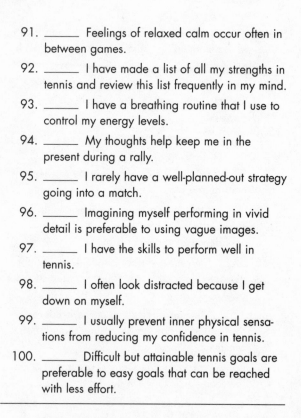

91. _____ Feelings of relaxed calm occur often in between games.
92. _____ I have made a list of all my strengths in tennis and review this list frequently in my mind.
93. _____ I have a breathing routine that I use to control my energy levels.
94. _____ My thoughts help keep me in the present during a rally.
95. _____ I rarely have a well-planned-out strategy going into a match.
96. _____ Imagining myself performing in vivid detail is preferable to using vague images.
97. _____ I have the skills to perform well in tennis.
98. _____ I often look distracted because I get down on myself.
99. _____ I usually prevent inner physical sensations from reducing my confidence in tennis.
100. _____ Difficult but attainable tennis goals are preferable to easy goals that can be reached with less effort.

Congratulations on completing the TMBC! (You have completed it, haven't you? If not, please do so before reading the scoring key that follows.) Your efforts at self-discovery will definitely pay off. Now, let's take a look at your results.

Scoring Part I

The first step in scoring the TMBC is to calculate your ACES profile. Give yourself one point for each response that matches the key, and enter the total for each dimension on the appropriate line below. Maximum score is 15 in each dimension.

Key for Dimension A

Answer True: 14, 28, 39, 42, 61, 67, 93, 97
Answer False: 4, 15, 30, 54, 59, 82, 98
Total Matches for A = ______

Key for Dimension C

Answer True: 18, 31, 33, 63, 70, 71, 88, 92, 94
Answer False: 13, 22, 32, 36, 74, 95
Total Matches for C = ______

Key for Dimension E

Answer True: 1, 9, 26, 34, 41, 43, 52, 87, 91
Answer False: 10, 23, 55, 58, 78, 84
Total Matches for E = ______

Key for Dimension S

Answer True: 2, 11, 44, 47, 76, 83, 99
Answer False: 7, 17, 21, 24, 50, 53, 65, 90
Total Matches for S = ______
Enter the scores below for your ACES profile:

A ______ (Actions/Behavior)
C ______ (Cognitions/Thoughts)
E ______ (Emotions/Feelings)
S ______ (Physical Sensations/Physiology)

Scoring Part II

The second step in scoring is to calculate your scores in five primary skill areas. Again, give yourself one point for each response that matches the key and enter the total for each skill area on the appropriate line. Maximum score is 20 for each area.

Key for Attention Control

Answer True: 1, 14, 28, 42, 47, 52, 63, 70, 83, 91, 94
Answer False: 7, 13, 21, 23, 32, 59, 78, 90, 98
Total Matches for Attention Control = ______

Key for Imagery

Answer True: 6, 19, 37, 51, 56, 57, 62, 68, 89, 96
Answer False: 5, 12, 27, 29, 38, 46, 69, 75, 77, 80
Total Matches for Imagery = ______

Key for Confidence

Answer True: 2, 9, 33, 34, 39, 43, 71, 92, 97, 99
Answer False: 15, 22, 24, 53, 54, 58, 65, 82, 84, 95
Total Matches for Confidence = ______

Key for Energy Control

Answer True: 11, 18, 26, 31, 41, 44, 61, 67, 76, 87, 88, 93
Answer False: 4, 10, 17, 30, 36, 50, 55, 74
Total Matches for Energy Control = ______

Key for Goal Setting

Answer True: 3, 40, 45, 48, 72, 73, 79, 81, 85, 100
Answer False: 8, 16, 20, 25, 35, 49, 60, 64, 66, 86
Total Matches for Goal Setting = ______

Enter scores below for your Skills profile:
A _____ (Attention Control)
I _____ (Imagery)
C _____ (Confidence)
E _____ (Energy Control)
G _____ (Goal Setting)

Interpreting Your Results

The self-discovery really begins now as you calculate your ACES Profile, Skills Profile, and Need Type.

ACES Profile

Take a look at your ACES Profile. Which type of expression received the lowest score? This is the type of expression that you want to improve most as you apply the techniques from *Smart Tennis.*

Here are some general guidelines for interpreting particular scores on ACES: 13–15 (Strong), 10–12 (Needs Improvement), 7–9 (Needs Major Improvement), 6 and below (Deficient).

Skills Profile

Now look at your Skills Profile. Which mind-body skill had the lowest score? Place initial emphasis on this skill by focusing strongly on the appropriate chapter: (A—Chapter Two, I—Chapter Three, C—Chapter Four, E—Chapter Five, G—Chapter Six).

Here are some general guidelines for interpreting particular scores on Skills: 17–20 (Strong), 13–16 (Needs Improvement), 9–12 (Needs Major Improvement), 8 and below (Deficient).

Finding Your Need Type

Take your lowest score on the ACES Profile and combine it with your lowest score on your Skills Profile to determine your Need Type. For example, if your lowest score on your ACES profile is E (Emotions) and your lowest score on the Skills profile is C (Confidence), your Need Type is E-C (Emotions and Confidence). You may have more than one Need Type if you have identical scores on either the ACES Profile or the Skills Profile.

Enter your Need Type (or Types) here:

_______ - _______ //_______ - _______

(ACES) (SKILL) (ACES) (SKILL)

The following sections list the twenty Need Types and a brief explanation to guide your development into a smart tennis player. Find your current Need Type (or Types) and then read the brief description given here.

A-A (Actions and Attention)

You should develop new behaviors that increase your level of concentration throughout a match. For example, you might perform a specific routine to maintain focus such as directing attention to the racket strings before receiving service. Pay close attention to Chapter Two!

A-I (Actions and Imagery)

You would benefit by managing your on-court behavior more effectively, and this is facilitated through imagery. The connection between imagery of events and actual behavior is strong. Imagine perfect performances more frequently. You will find help for this in Chapter Three!

A-C (Actions and Confidence)

You should discover ways to behave with more confidence on the court. For example, walk with your head upright regardless of the score and never give your opponent a confidence boost by appearing down. Acting confident is a must and leads to feelings, thoughts, and physical sensations of confidence too. Make sure to read Chapter Four for improvement in this area!

A-E (Actions and Energy)

You should find ways of acting to increase or decrease arousal so as to maintain optimal energy balance. For example, if you become overexcited, you might develop a deep breathing routine to lower arousal. If you lack energy, you might jog in place for a moment to fire yourself up. Refer to Chapter Five for assistance in this area!

A-G (Actions and Goal Setting)

You would gain from unlocking the powerful effects of goal setting, targeting specific behaviors both on and off the court. First identify actions needing change, and then monitor your improvement through video analysis or an outside observer. Pay close attention to Chapter Six!

C-A (Cognitions and Attention)

You should pay attention to the relationship between your thoughts and your ability to concentrate on the court. For example, thinking of past mistakes or worrying about match outcome only derails your focus. Try to stay "in the moment" as much as you can. You will find help for this in Chapter Two!

C-I (Cognitions and Imagery)

You should carefully monitor your thoughts and self-statements, and imagery is a great place to make improvements. For example, self-defeating or irrelevant thoughts during a match should be replaced with more positive self-statements through frequent imagery. Make sure to read Chapter Three for improvement!

C-C (Cognitions and Confidence)

You should more closely monitor your thinking patterns and how these influence your confidence. For example, if you attribute your losses to poor skill, it might help to discover another explanation such as your opponent's strength or your own inadequate preparation. Thoughts and confidence go hand in hand. Refer to Chapter Four for assistance in this area!

C-E (Cognitions and Energy)

You should focus on how your thinking patterns relate to your energy level on the court. For example, fatigue often leads to negative thinking in the final set. In this case, it helps to repeat energizing words to yourself such as "excitement" or "charge." You will find help for this in Chapter Five!

C-G (Cognitions and Goal Setting)

You would benefit from understanding how your attitudes and thoughts affect your performance on the court. With this knowledge, goal setting might be used not only to improve your physical performance but also to improve your thoughts and attitudes. Pay close attention to Chapter Six!

E-A (Emotions and Attention)

You should realize that optimal focus involves a relatively steady and positive flow of emotions throughout the match. For example, too much fear or anger will often distract you by narrowing your attentional focus. You might practice increasing concentration through emotionally charged situations. Make sure to read Chapter Two for improvement!

E-I (Emotions and Imagery)

You should use imagery to gain better insight into your feelings in a variety of situations. After identifying areas needing improvement, it helps to create an imagery script involving perfectly executed shots and optimal management of your feelings in a variety of situations. Refer to Chapter Three for assistance in this area!

E-C (Emotions and Confidence)

You should examine your feelings on the court and how they affect your expectations for success. For example, after winning an important game, you might be elated and need to guard against overconfidence. If you lack confidence, you might re-create feelings you had during previous successes. You will find help for this in Chapter Four!

E-E (Emotions and Energy)

You should closely monitor your feelings and arousal levels throughout the match. For example, during important points, you might get so excited that fine muscle coordination and your ability to make difficult shots decreases. Staying level-headed maintains energy balance and increases consistency. Pay close attention to Chapter Five!

E-G (Emotions and Goal Setting)

You should take advantage of goal setting, especially to ensure that feelings are not sabotaging your tennis performance. Emotions may change rapidly throughout a match. By monitoring and adjusting your feelings through goal setting, you will attain greater control and more success. Make sure to read Chapter Six!

S-A (Sensations and Attention)

You should pay closer attention to your internal bodily sensations and how these sensations affect your concentration. For example, you might find that your focus decreases if you don't experience a slight rush of adrenaline before the match. Study the relationship between physical sensations, concentration, and performance. Refer to Chapter Two for assistance!

S-I (Sensations and Imagery)

You should monitor your body's internal sensations in a variety of different scenarios and against different opponents. Then use imagery to re-create the sensations most associated with success. This reinforces the connection between positive mental and physical states, making these responses more likely in the future. You will find help for this in Chapter Three!

S-C (Sensations and Confidence)

You should examine how physical sensations relate to your level of confidence. For example, slight butterflies in your stomach might increase or decrease your expectations of success. Find out which sensations work best for you. It is then important to re-create these sensations for more confident performances. Pay close attention to Chapter Four!

S-E (Sensations and Energy)

You should learn your body's physiological reaction to a variety of situations. Being either too excited or too calm is often a problem. You'll find that it's useful to adjust physical sensations and energy levels with psych-up or psych-down techniques as needed. Make sure to read Chapter Five!

S-G (Sensations and Goal Setting)

You might find that physical sensations keep you from playing your best. One way of improving is to commit yourself to a few explicit performance goals. Clearly defined objectives free your mind of worry and change the way you interpret these sensations. The result is less stress and better play. Refer to Chapter Six for assistance!

Moving Forward

Now that you've calculated your ACES Profile, Skills Profile, and Need Type, you are well on your way toward becoming a Smart Tennis player. Write down your Need Type (or Types) and the corresponding notes for improvement on a small sheet of paper or index card. Keep these notes handy as you play tennis and gain even further self-awareness. Refer back to these notes as you read the book and your game evolves. Also use them to set performance goals, discussed in Chapter Six.

Subsequent chapters will provide you direction to improve in your identified areas of weakness and further enhance your areas of strength. You will learn a variety of techniques and strategies to lift your mind-body skills to a higher level. Regarding confidence, for example, how do you keep your confidence up when you are in a slump? How do you keep from choking on important points? I use real-life examples from experiences with my students and clients as well as research on these principles to illustrate effective techniques.

After your game has improved (and a couple of months of practice), go in for another checkup by taking the TMBC again. See how your Need Type has changed. At this point, you will learn even more about yourself and areas needing continued refinement. Reread appropriate chapters and see your smart tennis game improve again. Your ACES Profile, Skills Profile, and Need Type always help you know where to place your energies. As you can tell, this is a very exciting personal journey!

Begin by reading the chapter indicated by your Need Type. For example, if your first Need Type is E-E (Emotions and Energy), you would begin reading Chapter Three. Reading the whole book first is also fine, but remember to pay special attention to the chapter indicated by your Need Type.

Chapter Two introduces the fundamental mind-body skill of attention control. I've placed this topic next because it's fundamental in tennis, a sport that makes incredible attentional demands.

2

Attention Control

Staying Focused

Alicia, a fifteen-year-old Junior tennis competitor was walking to the court with her doubles partner, Gail. They'd just had a pre-match "chalk talk" with their coach, and Alicia was trying to concentrate on the coach's reminders about staying focused during their forthcoming match. Alicia took her coach's advice to heart. She'd shown a lot of tennis promise with consistent play the year before, but lately hadn't been playing very well. She thought that the cause of her recent problems was an inability to filter out distractions. She felt some confidence that if she could get into a serious yet relaxed state of mind prior to the match, and if she just recalled the simple pointers their coach had just shared with them, she would be able to maintain a fairly consistent and positive pattern of play. As she tried to review the coach's words, however, she was already becoming sidetracked by Gail's constant talking. When Gail realized that Alicia was not paying total attention to her, she talked louder and actually gave her a little shove.

Alicia focused her attention on Gail for the rest of the walk across the park to the court where their opponents were warming up. By the time she got to the court, she was totally confused about how to play her match. Even as they began hitting ground strokes with the other girls prior to the match, Gail kept talking to her. Suddenly, frustrated by her inability to do any mental rehearsal of the match she was about to play, Alicia yelled at Gail to shut up, and she walked off the court to try to recompose herself.

Alicia was still pretty upset when she started to serve in the first game. She was unable to relax her muscles and hit several double faults en route to losing the first game. As she changed courts between games, she was in tears. Her coach had been keeping a fairly close watch on Alicia because he knew that something was interfering with her tennis performance. He'd arrived at the court just in time to witness the blowup with Gail. It was obvious to him that Gail was interfering with Alicia's pre-match preparation program. Although Gail needed to talk to rid herself of precompetitive anxiety, doing so with Alicia was not helpful to her partner.

At their next match, the coach instructed Gail to talk only with him during the twenty to thirty minutes prior to the first match and to communicate with Alicia sparingly during the match—and only if it dealt with strategy. Alicia, meanwhile, was instructed to walk to the court alone, to make sure she went over the match in her head, and to keep her attention clear and focused as she started the match. Without distractions, Alicia was able to focus on the task-relevant information as it unfolded during the match. From that point onward, Alicia was able to compete at her best.

Alicia's performance was tied directly to her ability to maintain proper attention control. It's not by chance that I've placed attention control first in this journey toward becoming a smart tennis player. In my work with tennis players, I've found that proper attentional focus is the most important yet most elusive mind-body skill to master. Lose your concentration for just a brief moment and you might forfeit an important advantage. Focus too intensely and the same result is inevitable. Just as essential as precise strokes and physical fitness, attention control is absolutely vital in the sport of tennis.

> You could set off dynamite in the next court and I wouldn't notice.
>
> —Maureen Connolly, three-time Wimbledon champion

Unforced errors caused by distractions are all too frequent in this sport where consistency rules. These distractions take many forms and wreak havoc among players at every level. One top-ranked collegiate tennis player I recently worked with described her struggle with attention control in these terms:

I dwell on past mistakes and think too much about the score and what's going to happen next. As my heart races I become distracted and fearful, overly careful with my shots, and I find it hard to return to the present.

It is important to note that poor attention control for this player led to problems in all areas of expression including thoughts (past or present events), feelings (anxiety), actions (conservative play), and physical sensations (racing heart). Just as one bad apple will spoil a whole barrel, one recurring mind-body flaw (poor concentration, for example) often has disastrous consequences in your overall play.

After this player took the TMBC from Chapter One and applied the principles from *Smart Tennis* to focus more effectively, problems resolved in all four modes of expression. She began noticing improvements in her attention control and match results improved too. Identifying poor concentration as the source of a dangerous domino effect was half the battle for her.

Players and coaches at all levels often mistakenly assume that attention control is just a function of thoughts and perceptions. People often forget that proper attention is determined by many other factors too, including physical arousal level, specific activity engaged in, and emotional state. The key is to screen out distractions while allowing into your awareness only those items that will enhance your focus. This is an exciting topic that should not be oversimplified!

Types of Attentional Focus

Research into the nature of attentional focus indicates that there are four different types of attentional focus organized along two dimensions, broad and narrow. Players shift between these different types of focus throughout a match depending on changing situations. Let's examine these different types of attentional focus.

- *Broad focus:* A broad attentional focus allows you to recognize multiple elements in the environment simultaneously. This keeps you from becoming so narrowly focused that you miss important elements. One reason why coaches should not overuse the phrase "watch the ball" in their instruction is that it detracts from this broad focus.
- *Narrow focus:* A narrow attentional focus allows you to focus on fewer cues. For example, before

serving, you narrow focus to foot position, to the toss, and then to the ball. After serving, you shift focus again to a broader view.

- *External focus:* An external attentional focus allows you to direct attention outward to objects in the environment. For example, in setting up to hit an overhead smash, you retrieve back while targeting the rising ball with the opposite hand.
- *Internal focus:* An internal attentional focus puts you in touch with inner thoughts, feelings, and sensations. For example, during changeovers, you might prepare a strategy. In the midst of a long rally, you might visualize a particular shot sequence. Exhibit 2.1 illustrates how these four types of attentional focus combine to handle the varied demands of tennis.

Problems with Attention

Since attention control is such an important factor in playing smart tennis, it's also important to recognize how it can go wrong. Three problems with attention occur more often than we'd like to admit. Take a look and see if you can relate to any of these problems.

Excessive Stress

Although Chapter Five takes up the topic more completely, stress is relevant here, too. States such as stress,

Exhibit 2.1
Examples of Combinations of Attentional Focus in Tennis

Broad-External	*Broad-Internal*
Awareness of court positioning, ball, and opponent positioning	Thinking about general match strategy
Narrow-External	*Narrow-Internal*
Visual awareness of the ball prior to hitting an overhead smash	Using imagery to simulate a specific situation or positive emotional state

Source: Nideffer, 1981. Reprinted by permission.

anxiety, and high arousal directly alter the width and quality of attention. Excessive stress and anxiety make it much more difficult to maintain proper attention control.

Worry and fear are examples of stressful internal states that will distract you from your best concentration. These distractions reduce task-focus, leading to inevitable performance declines. In addition to cluttering the mind with needless thoughts and worries, players under excessive stress experience a narrowing of attentional focus. Perceptually, this narrowing is like playing a match with blinders on or viewing the court through a narrow tube. With focus narrowed, you miss important elements in your environment. These

Figure 2.1
An Overly Narrow Attentional Focus

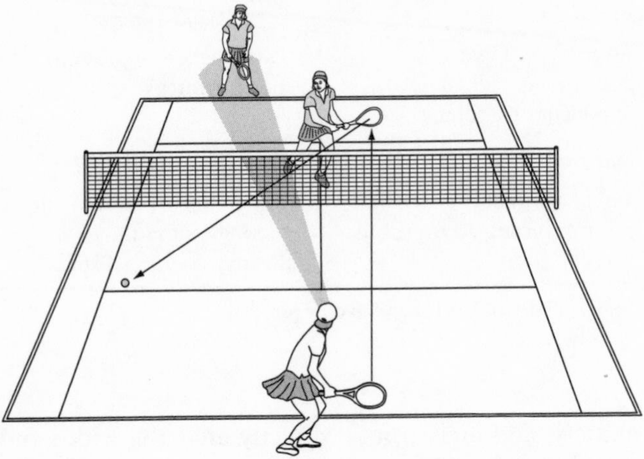

may include visual or auditory signals that the opponent is rushing the net, or other cues that would normally help you predict your opponent's next shot. Figure 2.1 shows what might happen with an overly narrow focus.

Choking

Choking in tennis is often described as a deficit in attention, but very little research has examined this process. It is a process involving several factors that result in poor play. Circumstances that precede choking may include perceptions that the point or match is extremely important, excessive self-consciousness, attention drawn inward, or a sense of being evaluated by others. Too much importance placed on one situation evokes thoughts and memories of past failure or negative what-if scenarios. The cumulative result of this process is distraction from the task at hand. Players who choke experience difficulty shifting attention rapidly and smoothly and often remain fixated too long with a narrow and internal focus.

In addition to changes in direction of focus, physiological changes make it more probable that errors will occur. For example, anxiety might cause sweaty palms and impair racket control, tension could destroy fine muscular coordination, and an increased breathing rate could make oxygen exchange difficult, leading to fatigue and discomfort. Given all these effects, it's amazing that players can ever keep it together under pressure! Applying the principles of attention control in this chapter will greatly reduce your tendency to choke.

Being Overly Relaxed

Although stress and worry are thought of as destroying attention, you need some level of stress to avoid the opposite effect of becoming too relaxed. When this happens, your attention expands so broadly that elements having no value to your success as a tennis player find their way into your consciousness. Focus on the important elements is shared with irrelevant items and

Figure 2.2
An Overly Broad Attentional Focus

attention control is lost. For example, an overly relaxed player might pause to hear the sound of the crowd and lose an attentional edge for the rest of the match. Figure 2.2 illustrates the problem you might run into with an overly broad focus.

The general effects of stress on attention are shown in Figure 2.3. Note that your stress level directly influences the width of attention. Your goal in attention control is to discover an optimal focus that admits relevant stimuli while blocking out distractions.

Selective Attention and Concentration

If you've focused long enough to reach this point, you're on your way toward gaining the attention control of a champion. Let's begin by discussing two important elements of attention control, selective attention and concentration. Later on, you'll be provided more specific strategies to improve this mind-body skill.

> She played tennis the way an orchestra plays Beethoven, deftly, lovingly, but with intense concentration on the notes.
>
> —Jim Murray, on Chris Evert

We are constantly bombarded by an endless array of internal and external stimuli, thoughts, and emotions. Given this abundance of data, it's amazing that we make sense of anything! In varying degrees of efficiency, we have developed the

Figure 2.3
Effects of Stress on Attention

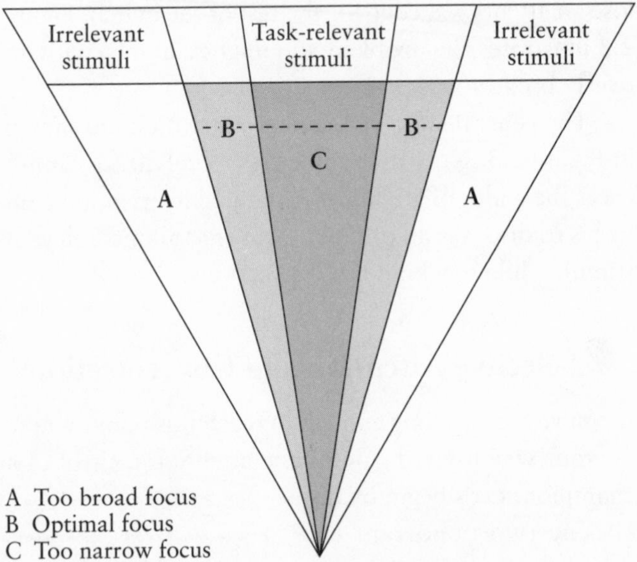

A Too broad focus
B Optimal focus
C Too narrow focus

Source: Martens, 1987, p. 145. Reprinted by permission.

ability to direct our attention to what is important while blocking out the rest. This process of focusing our awareness on relevant stimuli while ignoring irrelevant stimuli is termed *selective attention.* Maintaining this attention control over an extended period of time is called *concentration.*

Many sport psychologists believe that selective attention is the most important mental characteristic of

Figure 2.4
Shifting Between the Four Different Types of Attentional Focus

successful athletic performance. Selective attention requires you to shift attention, as in Figure 2.4, between the four different types of focus previously discussed. Your brain does this naturally, but increased awareness of the process is the first step in discovering ways of improving attention control as needed.

Here is an example of how the process of attentional shift works. You walk onto the court for warm-ups with a broad-external focus. You take in all elements of the external environment and scan with your senses to become comfortable with the setting. Perhaps the wind is blowing in a particular direction or the sun affects only one side of the court. During the warm-up, you shift to a broad-internal focus as you recall the last time you faced this opponent. You scan your memory for what worked in the past and devise a specific plan for that day. The focus becomes narrow-internal as you use imagery to anticipate a particular shot sequence and elicit feelings of relaxed confidence prior to serving. Your focus again becomes broad-external as the point develops and you open your awareness fully to the rally. The focus then quickly becomes narrow-external as you move in to hit a precise counter drop shot to win the point.

In addition to shifting focus effectively through selective attention, you need to be able to sustain attention throughout the point and match with concentration. Take care, however, to relax attention following points, games, and matches. Just as careless attention leaves you vulnerable to many irrelevant internal and external factors (such as negative thoughts or the sight of players on nearby courts), overly intense concentration reduces sharpness and may leave you fatigued. This overintensity is also what happens when you choke, as discussed earlier. Frequent breaks in concentration are as healthy and necessary in tennis as in study—focusing too long on one thing at a time reduces performance efficiency and causes boredom and fatigue.

Increasing the length of time you can effectively concentrate is the mind-body equivalent of developing consistency and physical stamina in tennis. Hitting more balls over the net without making mistakes is just as important as increasing the time you can remain optimally attentive to the proper elements on the court. Tennis is a game of unforced errors, so the ability to concentrate longer than your opponent wins you more points. And since attention is an internal process, it does not reveal itself easily to the opponent, making it even more effective. Concentration is even more important to your success than a big serve or backhand passing shot, and your opponent often fails to realize your improvement until it's much too late! Now let's take it a step further by describing the quality of optimal attention control.

Finding Your Zone

Although gaining attention control might appear to involve great strain and exertion, the opposite is actually true. Effective concentration has been described as effortless effort, being "in the zone," a flow state, and a passive process of being totally absorbed in the present and fascinated by the object of fixation.

Many tennis players have spoken about "the zone"

and most agree that it's a great place to be. What exactly is this zone? The zone is difficult to describe because it reflects an ideal performance state involving little conscious control or analytical thought. The feeling in the zone, however, is one of pure enjoyment and effectiveness. It is a sense of complete satisfaction and absorption in the present moment and a feeling of natural power. In the zone, attention is so efficient that the mind and body act together like one integrated unit on automatic pilot. This is actually the unifying theme of the smart tennis approach. Mind and body are really one and should act as such!

Although the zone is a desirable place to be, human beings usually grunt and groan and stumble around for quite a while before they ever realize the value of finding it. Since much analysis often goes into discovering a new process, this is not entirely surprising. Overanalysis, judgment, and criticism, however, close the door to the zone. As a smart tennis player, you should be actively involved in learning the mind-body skills and applying them to your game. Since learning is an ongoing process involving reflection, correction, and adaptation, you cannot be in the zone all the time! If it were that easy, there would be no need to read this book. You could just book your flight to Wimbledon.

Nevertheless, it's a very good idea to take the time to figure out how to open the door to the zone. Here are some tips to help you achieve this state of inner calm and security more often. Begin by allowing your instincts to rule. Spend time on the court and off the court just experiencing tennis, withholding all judgment. After selecting a strategy, hit the ball without any conscious effort. Play like a free animal, fully in tune with your senses and fully enjoying the sport. Play a whole set with these principles in mind, refraining from any judgment at all about how well you are performing. Relax, let go, and allow the mechanics of tennis to take care of themselves. Combine your relaxed and effortless style of play with solid tennis fundamentals and you will discover the zone more frequently, allowing smart tennis to rule.

Staying Thrilled in the Zone

The problem with the zone is that it's very elusive. Just when you think you are in the zone, it slips away! One way to make the zone a more permanent residence on the tennis court—and in your head—is to stay thrilled with what you are doing. This fascination with the moment is really the hallmark of proper attention. Think back to the last time you were completely absorbed in the moment during a point. You probably recall very few details because you were so focused and excited to just play tennis. Your focus left you no energy for self-consciousness, worry, or analysis. The key point is that you were thrilled with your tennis and had no time or energy to devote to anything but performance.

Excitement with the present moment is much more effective than straining to watch the ball or hold your mind punitively on a task with bulging facial muscles. That's why I cringe when inexperienced tennis coaches yell at their students to "watch the ball." That phrase is really overworked and meaningless. What all tennis players need is a way of enjoying the process more so that their focus comes to them naturally. Was it difficult to stay focused on the best day of tennis in your life? If you are a beginner, think of another performance situation. Of course is was not hard; it came naturally! Straining for focus is maladaptive. If you can evoke feelings of being thrilled, there is no need for your attention to stray; you stay in the zone. Like any finely tuned skill, it takes practice and patience to develop a consistent excited awareness for optimal attention control. Just remember that staying "thrilled in the zone" is a joyful absorption in the present rather than an effortful struggle.

The Orienting Response

Concentration is a very difficult skill to acquire and master because your mind tends to shift focus whenever presented with novel stimuli. Known as the *orienting response,* the natural human bias toward new sights and sounds alerted our ancestors to dangers in the wild—where sudden changes often signaled something deadly. This same survival mechanism unfortunately leaves us victim to meaningless distractions on the tennis court. A split-second loss of concentration during a critical point will not kill you—but it may spell the difference between winning and losing. Careful planning and practice are required to gain supremacy over your attentional faculties. Fortunately, selective attention and concentration are skills that can be learned, refined, and perfected just like volleys and drop shots. Since few players devote time to attentional skills, there is an immediate and tangible reward for those who do! I believe the struggle with oneself over attentional control is even more fundamental than the clash with the opponent, for only after monitoring and adjusting our own level of focus are we ready to use this skill as a real weapon on the court.

Let's move now from theory to practice, and I mean that literally! Just as it's important to understand attention control, it is equally necessary to take action to enhance concentration. The ensuing sections help you take this mind-body skill to a new level.

Getting Serious About Practice

The first step in gaining supreme attention control is to put on your focus cap whenever you pick up a tennis racket. This applies whether you are playing at Wimbledon or practicing against your garage door. Unfortunately, many players just go through the motions in practice, hoping to magically wake up and display their true stardom once they reach Wimbledon. This type of practice would be better spent cleaning out the garage or dusting off old trophies. True competitors make their practices as worthwhile as their matches, collecting new trophies along the way.

Make attention control a hallmark of your practice sessions. Develop the attitude that practice is the most decisive factor of the match. For the smart tennis player, there is simply no substitute for smart practice. Mind-body strategies and techniques used in a tournament are firmly established in these previews. The ebb and flow of a match, like the weather, is usually difficult to predict. This very exciting aspect of tennis is also quite dangerous since control and consistency are your main allies.

Simulation

Simulation is a term often used by sport psychologists to refer to realistic practice. The objective is to re-create the experience of competition in practice so that you are ready when it really counts. This involves setting up practices that lead to the same pressure (or close to it) that you experience in the match. Start by finding a partner equally motivated to practice smart. Observe all qualities of attention control in both yourself and your opponent. Spend time discussing how well you focused that day, and the skill of attention control will come to life. You will recognize attention control in all dimensions. Recognizing lapses in attention will make your determination for improvement and sense of direction increase.

If you have time to scout your opponent prior to the big match, simulate shots that would work best for you against that player's weakness. Next, practice situations in which your opponent's strength is played to your weakness. I'm sure you can come up with many other creative simulations that have the effect of forcing you to concentrate for extended periods of time. The challenge is to make it seem realistic. Use lots of variety throughout the session and remain completely focused. Play out points exactly as you would in the match. Your practices will take on a rich dimension and you'll be prepared as never before.

Create Distractions in Practice

Simulation training requires that you prepare for any eventuality. This may include noises, thoughts, images or internal sensations. To the degree that you are able to produce these distractions in practice, you will be prepared to meet them head on in the game. Tennis has noble roots with a strong emphasis on protocol and etiquette. Unlike people in many team sports, tennis players didn't usually have to learn to deal with rowdy crowds or vicious insults. Although hitting a baseball is as technically demanding as hitting a tennis ball, baseball players are required to block out distractions all the time. Since tennis players are naturally inclined to be more sensitive to distractions, extra work in this area helps a lot.

Realize that distractions need not come in only the baseball or football variety. Weather conditions, mind games, fatigue, and anxiety should be motivation enough to realize that distraction blocking is a worthy venture. Figure out what is bothering you in your game and set out to conquer this problem by meeting it squarely on the practice court. Simulation training means setting up conditions that you will face in the game. Another bonus is that dealing with distractions in practice prevents boredom because your activities are realistic, practical, and challenging.

Overlearning in Practice

Another very useful way of enhancing attention control in competitive situations is to overlearn skills that you already possess. Think for a moment about your greatest strength. It may be your forehand, your strategic prowess, or your confidence. Now take that skill and drill it over and over in practice. You might spend an extra fifteen minutes just going over the same routine or eliciting the same mental state during practice. There is research to suggest that the repetition of overlearning makes attention control more automatic. I always find that it helps to overlearn several key skills before every match. Practicing what you already know to the point of overlearning frees your mind and makes the process of selecting and shifting attention smoother.

Using Self-Talk for Attention Control

Language may be the most powerful tool ever invented to influence behavior. Language directed inward, or *self-talk,* is especially important in performance situations. Sport psychologists describe self-talk as thinking or making internal or external statements about personal performance. This dialogue with oneself provides a means of identifying and solving problems by making perceptions and beliefs conscious. On the tennis court, the quality of self-talk needs to be carefully scrutinized to ensure a mental state where optimal performance can flourish and negativity is extinguished.

The influence of self-talk on performance has been demonstrated across a variety of sports. Available research indicates that self-talk can improve attention control and create positive expectancies. Positive self-talk has also been associated with more successful competitive outcomes whereas negative self-talk is associated with losing and poorer attention control. Self-talk is also an effective tool to enhance many of the techniques discussed later in this book, including arousal management, competitive pressure management, anger management, elimination of fear and choking, and development of the killer instinct.

The ensuing advice introduces you to ways of identifying and modifying self-talk where appropriate. It should be emphasized, however, that every tennis player is a unique individual with internalized beliefs and assumptions reflected in self-talk. As such, improving self-talk often takes great insight, effort, and persistence.

Identifying Self-Talk

The content and context of self-talk must be first understood. As soon as possible following a match, make a list of your thoughts and self-statements, situations in which they occurred, and performance consequences. Recall your typical thinking and verbal reactions to a variety of performance situations. If possible, have someone videotape a tough match with close-ups of your facial expressions and verbalizations. This will further help you identify self-talk in various situations.

The following on-court technique is another way to help you identify negative self-talk and improve your attention to the internal dialogue. Place fifty paper clips in your right pocket prior to a match. Every time you make a negative self-statement, transfer one paper clip to the left pocket. At the end of the match, you may be shocked to see how many clips have gone to the left side! Set specific goals to reduce the number of paper clips in your left pocket each time you play. You will be amazed at what you learn about yourself!

Modifying Self-Talk

First determine whether you are really committed to eliminating negative self-talk. Without a full commitment, change for the better is unlikely. Interrupt negative self-talk as soon as it occurs with a positive visual image (say, see yourself holding up a trophy), phrase (such as "I'm getting better"), or action (perhaps a positively clenched fist). Negative self-talk often accumulates in a match and it is important to interrupt it before it interrupts you.

Whenever a negative self-statement crops up, replace it with a more constructive version. For example, change "I'm terrible" to "I love this challenge."

If you find that your attention is wandering, self-statements such as "stay here" or "now" help return your attention to the present moment. Self-talk can also be used to keep you focused on external cues such as the ball, or the intended direction of your shot, with phrases such as "set" or "cross."

Examine the beliefs underlying the content of your self-talk. You may discover that many of the assumptions that drive your self-talk are invalid. For example, the belief that you have to win every match or you are a bad player or poor competitor is simply wrong. Work on challenging and refuting negative and erroneous beliefs so that more constructive and positive self-talk emerges.

Your ability to remain positively focused and attentive to necessary stimuli is directly related to the quality of your self-talk and your capacity to modulate it as needed. After you have clearly identified this internal dialogue, changes are possible. Don't worry if people see you talking to yourself. Just tell them you're enjoying the conversation!

Improving Mental and Physical Quickness

In addition to remaining thrilled in the moment and focused completely on your task, attention control allows you to gain another major advantage—quickness!

If you would like to improve your overall quickness on the tennis court, there are some means available through improved conditioning, agility, and footwork. After that, you may need to choose faster parents to gain a sizable physical advantage, since genetic factors (such as the firing rate of muscle fibers) place an upper limit on your ability to move. What may surprise you is that quickness in tennis has less to do with raw speed—fast-twitch muscle fibers—and more to do with attention control skills!

Although physical proficiency is both desirable and necessary for high levels of play, mind-body superiority in the form of anticipatory skills is far more meaningful in achieving quickness in tennis. Visual scanning research in racket sports has shown that experts differ from novices in eye fixation patterns and perceptual strategies. For example, whereas experts focus consistently on cues presented by the opponent before something happens (the angle of the racket prior to contact, the position of the server's shoulder, and so on), novices display less controlled fixations and focus on cues that appear much later (such as the position of the ball after contact). The ability to attend to relevant early cues and interpret them accurately is the hallmark of superior anticipation—and therefore of superior quickness, because the sooner you know something is happening, the more effectively you can deal with it.

In short, tennis quickness involves being prepared, knowing what kind of shot to expect from early visual clues, and acting accordingly on that knowledge. If you have poor anticipatory skills and are constantly late in reacting to your opponent, your world-class speed will be useless. What is really exciting is that anticipatory skills in tennis can be practiced and improved. Tennis players can learn to make faster and more accurate decisions regarding the type and direction of shots following a mental quickness training program.

There are two areas of attention control where improvements will lead to enhanced anticipatory skills and greater tennis quickness. The first, already discussed, involves recognizing the meaning of appropriate early cues and implementing this knowledge in game situations. The second area is more traditional and involves reviewing the fine points of timing and court positioning as they relate to the type of shot hit, position of the player, and position of the opponent. While very few club players have mastered these skills, it's also true that many collegiate and professional players would benefit from refinement in this area as well.

Exercises to Improve Attention Control

By now you should be familiar with a variety of factors relating to maintaining proper attention control in tennis. This section presents a few exercises to help you further improve your attention control in tennis. Remember that the smart tennis player places just as much importance on these mind-body skills as on the more traditional activities such as improving shot placement and spin.

Develop a Consistent Routine

Elite athletes in all sports learn to develop a consistent routine or ritual both prior to and during performance. These routines do wonders for your attention control. In tennis, for example, players dress, stretch, and warm up in exactly the same way before every match. They practice other unique routines over and over throughout the match. For example, one player will bounce the ball three times and then one time before serving. Another player will tap his shoes with his racket three times before receiving serve. During changeovers, a third player will always hit the strings of the racket and place a towel over his head while visualizing the next game.

Consistent routines also help guard against the situational effects of stress by providing the player with a very comfortable and familiar mind-set. They also tend to make performance more automatic. Since automatic behaviors require little or no conscious attention, routines let you save more attention for the important tasks. Just like your computer programs, your mind-body skills work better when you have some extra hard drive space.

If you don't already have a unique and consistent routine that you use all the time, develop one now. If you have some routines but they are inconsistent, now is the time to make them more consistent. Develop a routine that is comfortable to you and write down all the steps in your routine. Pay conscious attention to your routine initially, and it will become more automatic as time goes on.

Thought Freezing

Since attention wanders so frequently, it is important to develop a mechanism of examining the contents of your focus in practice. Arrange a tennis drill in which you determine beforehand what kind of focus is necessary for optimal attention. For example, while practicing short cross-court volleys, a narrow-external focus on the path of the ball is required to execute the skill.

Next, have your partner shout out the word "freeze" at various unexpected points during the drill. At exactly the moment you hear the shout, stop what you are doing and quickly describe the contents of your focus to your partner. This exercise will put you more closely in touch with your thoughts, feelings, physical sensations, and activities while they really count! This is the best kind of simulation. Not only will you be determining the proper attentional focus needed for a particular task, you will also acquire feedback about your actual on-court attentional process. This exercise is really a lot of fun—and challenges your partner too! And shouting "freeze" for your partner lets you learn how others process information and exert attention control.

Build a Home on the Tennis Court

Just as a consistent routine is a behavioral means of achieving comfort and anxiety reduction, building a home on the tennis court serves a similar function in enhancing attention. Your home must be a place to go to frequently in times of need. Some players choose to mark off a 2' × 2' square on the clay court. Other players use a towel to construct their home. Wherever your home is on the court, go to it frequently in between points and during changeovers. It's a sanctuary where you know you're protected from all possible distractions. Having a home while your opponent is just wandering around on the other side of the court gives you an attentional edge!

Specific Tips for Improving Attention Control

Here are some specific tips to help you develop better attention control. Refer to this section often on the evening before or day of an important match so that they will remain fresh in your mind.

- Avoid negative thoughts and feelings—these are just needless distractions that rob you of your valuable attentional resources.
- Remain centered in the present, attending only to what is immediately important and blocking out past and future concerns. After a mistake, briefly note any changes necessary and then move decisively to the next point.
- Recite key words or phrases to yourself prior to the point to remind yourself to stay focused (such as "concentrate," "control," or "good contact").
- Be task rather than outcome oriented. Thinking about the score or how you look are common distractions. The outcome only improves when you ignore it and attend to what you have to do to succeed.

- Relax slightly between points, but avoid external distractions. Some players achieve this by practicing eye control. Focus on an object such as racket strings and vividly imagine the upcoming point.
- Be selfish with your attention. Keep to yourself and avoid talking to your opponent or the spectators during changeovers. This is your time to store up energy, sip water, and calmly regain your focus for the next game.
- Be particularly vigilant when physically or emotionally fatigued. Players often lose their focus when they get tired. Treat fatigue just like you would any other common distraction. Overcome fatigue with superior mind-body skills, including focused attention.
- Attention and arousal are closely related. Avoid becoming overly aroused while remaining focused on executing shots and implementing your strategy. Brief breathing and relaxation exercises can help lower arousal.
- Make practices fun by frequently changing the skills you practice and varying the routines. This will increase motivation, which also leads to improved attention control.
- During practice, see how long you can stay intensely focused on the game. Time yourself to gauge your span of attention. Set up drills that

force you to play consistent mind-body tennis and set goals to gain longer periods of proper focus.

Every challenge presents new opportunities. Developing fine attention control is one of the greatest challenges in the sport of tennis. Grasping the principles and applying the techniques from this chapter give you the opportunity to perform far beyond your current level. As you develop greater attention control, you'll find that you are more aware of subtle changes needed to advance even further. Go for the zone.

Chapter Three introduces the exciting mind-body skill of imagery. Imagery frees you from the bounds of space and time and allows you to improve your game even when you're on an airplane, hours from your next match.

3

Imagery

Your Mind-Body Time Machine

Mrs. Juanita Martinez wanted only the best for her seventeen-year-old son, José. She agonized over José's poor academic progress in school. He'd been diagnosed with a learning disorder in junior high, and he had a tough time studying or paying attention in class. His lack of confidence in school carried over into his out-of-school life. He needed to find something he was good at to help his confidence.

Without getting his approval, she enrolled him in a tennis clinic for beginners at a park near their south-central Los Angeles home. She bought a racket at a garage sale and encouraged him to go to the clinic.

Although reluctant at first, José eventually agreed to attend the clinic, and was surprised when the instructor, Jefferson Compton, complimented him on his natural eye-hand coordination and excellent speed. Throughout the summer he returned to the park and played tennis in Jefferson's park program. With Jefferson's guidance and encouragement, José made quick strides. It was Jefferson's opinion that José could make the high school tennis team the following spring. Because José's school experience had left him with little confidence or sense of self-worth, his success at tennis was a source of great satisfaction to him.

Some of his lack of confidence in academics carried over into tennis. He had most of his best practice sessions and matches when he did not think of anything and just responded to the unfolding situation on the court. José's strength was speed, but at times he had to slow down to avoid overrunning or overhitting his shots. Jefferson had tried to get him to use imagery to help him achieve better consistency and to respond calmly to match conditions. Because of his academic experiences, however, José just didn't think he would be any good at imagery or other types of mental skills.

He'd recently had a great match, which Jefferson had taped. As José watched the video, the tennis experience came flooding back to him. He was barely looking at the monitor, and actually felt pressure in his legs and the physical sensation of ball contact in his hitting arm as he watched the images on the screen.

Later Jefferson discussed the match with him. José had nearly perfect recall of every shot. After about half an hour of discussion Jefferson said, "José, you have an exceptionally accurate mental picture of the match. If you can do that, you can be successful at imagery. Let's try it and see how it works. This time we'll just start with the serve. As you get more confidence, we can gradually link the other aspects of play."

José's first tendency was to doubt his ability, but as he thought things through he realized that Jefferson was right. He had an incredible image of that match. Maybe he could learn to use imagery after all. "All right, I'll try," he said.

Encouraged by his mother and Jefferson, within three months José was consistently using imagery prior to, during, and after his tennis matches at the park. His tennis skills improved, and he entered a couple of tournaments in various parts of Los Angeles during the fall. His imagery skill with tennis had given him much more confidence in his ability to concentrate. He found that, although he was spending as much time playing tennis as studying, he was actually doing better in the classroom. He even thought that if he didn't make the tennis team in the spring, he could always concentrate on his schoolwork and maybe even go to college.

Playing tennis and using imagery helped José feel much better about himself and his future potential. Think of this chapter as your invitation to greater freedom too. Many tennis players that I work with become so absorbed with immediate concerns, fears, and worries that they disregard their best past performances or find it difficult to see possibilities for the future. Imagery is a fantastic mind-body tool because it frees you to explore your whole range of past, present, and future experiences, and lets you improve your game even when you're not on the court! It works wonders for players at all levels. Fortunately for you, most tennis players still do not understand or use imagery properly. This chapter shows you how to travel in time with style.

Whereas attention control (Chapter Two) kept you centered in the here and now, imagery gives you wings to navigate space and time as needed to improve your performance. Imagery applies to every aspect of performance; when you have mastered this chapter you will be able to use it to enhance all other mind-body techniques. Read and understand this chapter completely, however, or your performance could be diminished by using this tool improperly. There is no question that if you take a smart tennis approach to imagery you'll be a much better performer.

One college tennis player I worked with described the benefits of imagery a day after upsetting a nationally ranked rival:

It [imagery] familiarized me with the match so much that by the time I arrived on the courts I felt completely prepared. Very little surprised me because I had rehearsed these situations over and over. I stayed relaxed and played steady tennis and my thoughts were much clearer. This definitely put me in the frame of mind to perform my best.

The advantages of imagery could be seen in this player's actions (playing steady) thoughts (clearer, less surprised), feelings (prepared, confident), and physical sensations (relaxed). Benefits of his imagery could be seen across multiple domains. There were no quick solutions or trickery involved, just high-quality time spent discussing and practicing imagery. It was a regular part of his daily training.

One Division I college tennis team I recently consulted with began imaging a victory over their arch rival every night for four weeks prior to their match. They had lost their first match of the season against this opponent 3–6, but a win would send them to their first NCAA post-season tournament in school history. Players used prophetic imagery (discussed later) to visualize specific situations before, during, and after the match, including the next day's headlines announcing their

"6–3 victory." Players also signed a contract pledging to finish their season strong and reverse that earlier match with a 6–3 win. They went on to win the match 6–3, qualified for their first NCAA tournament, and had the best season in their history!

In a moment, you'll be introduced to this wonderful tool. Later, you'll see explicit instructions on how to prepare for and use imagery to make your time travel more rewarding.

Upgrade Your Software

Tennis is often called a "mental sport." What does this mean? In my opinion, it accents the demands placed upon the player. High priorities include having a well-rehearsed pre-match strategy, making rapid and accurate decisions under fire, adjusting as necessary, and staying calm and focused. It's much like playing chess, but a whole lot more fun and healthier for the body!

Smart tennis players realize that mental factors are also essential in developing physical tools for the game (efficient strokes, proper footwork, fitness), for without effective instruction and knowledge, progress is difficult. The psychological demands of tennis require that mind-body tools be well developed. Unlike in some other sports, sheer athletic ability and brute strength are not the most important factors. What is really needed in tennis is more advanced software for your mind-body system. This software is imagery.

Imagery Defined

Imagery, also called mental rehearsal, mental practice, or visualization, is the process of creating or re-creating an experience in the mind in the absence of external stimuli. Whenever you imagine yourself performing an action in the absence of physical practice, you are using imagery. The goal is to make imagery seem as realistic as possible by using as many modes of expression as possible. Although the word *imagery* implies vision—mental pictures—let's use this term more broadly to include the simulation of anything that will improve your game: sound, smell, touch, taste, body awareness, emotions, thoughts, actions, internal sensations, even psychological states such as confidence and focus. Figure 3.1 illustrates the various modes of imagery. Clearly, your imagery time machine is an instrument with advanced capabilities!

> I see one coming and visualize where I'm going to hit it, and the shot's perfect—and I feel beautiful all over.
>
> —Billie Jean King, on making a great shot

Although research into the merits and workings of imagery lags behind the practice of the technique, many

Figure 3.1
The Many Expressions of Imagery

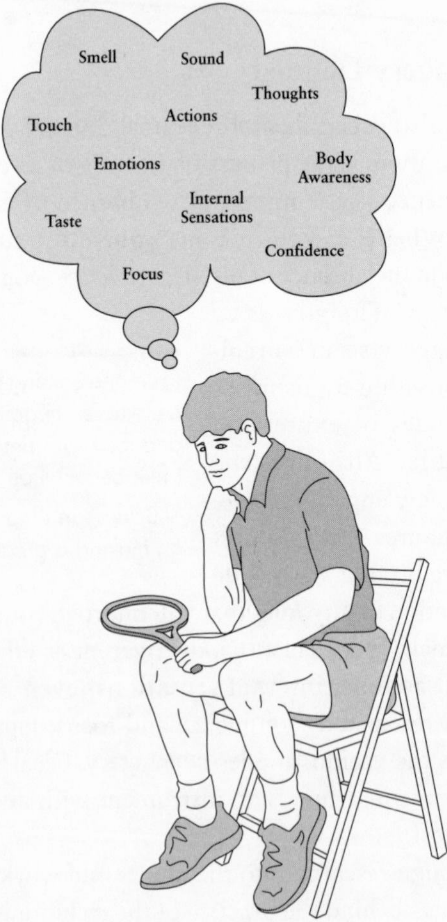

tennis players find imagery helpful. They use it for rehearsing new skills, practicing and refining existing skills, preparing for particular points, and readying for an entire match. Studies have shown imagery to be helpful in a variety of ways such as reducing warm-up decrement, lowering anxiety, and increasing self-confidence. Research shows that imagery alone is better than no practice at all, and that imagery combined with physical practice is better than either alone.

Regular Mental and Physical Training

Like any important skill, imagery requires consistent and correct practice. Most tennis players spend enormous amounts of time and energy on strokes and other physical skills while neglecting mind-body skills such as visualization. Ask yourself what percentage of your practice time is spent hitting balls versus developing and training essential mind-body skills such as imagery. You are selling yourself short if you give too little attention to this essential performance tool.

As suggested earlier, imagery may hurt your game if your understanding of strategy or strokes is deficient. Imaging poor technique only reinforces bad habits. Before getting started, make sure your knowledge and basic skills are up to the job. If you are an advanced tennis player, this should pose few difficulties. Beginners and intermediates might want to schedule a few lessons with their local professional to correct faulty technique. Players at all levels fail to progress from year to year either because they do not understand their weaknesses or because they know their limitations but cannot make necessary changes! The old saying "practice makes perfect" is quite misleading. Actually, practice makes *permanent*. Only perfect practice makes perfect! This applies to imagery as well.

Find a tennis professional who knows the game well, communicates this knowledge effectively, and keeps up with the latest developments. Check for professional credentials. The best pros are certified by major tennis teaching organizations such as the United States Professional Tennis Association and the United States Professional Tennis Registry, or an associated organization outside the United States. Read about the game, attend camps and seminars, play tournaments, and bring your knowledge back to your lessons. Dare your mentor to come up with a better mousetrap for you, and challenge yourself by asking good questions and keeping notes. I'm sure your pro will enjoy your lust for the game!

Advanced Software Is Really Simple

In this age of multimedia, athletes are more than ever bombarded with advice and instructions for improvement. There always seems to be another expert around the corner waiting to enlighten you. The beauty of imagery is that, although it may seem complex, it demands only that you summon up the rich imagination you had as a child. The world of the possible comprises vivid images and multidimensional sensations. Verbal instruction doesn't come close to matching the impact of an imagined experience. So before you update your mind-body software with imagery, free your hard drive of overdeveloped rules, restrictions, and analysis. Allow yourself to possess the creative imagination of a child, and tune in once again to the most advanced computer yet developed: your brain.

How Imagery Works in Tennis

Let's take a step back and examine some explanations given for how this brilliant tool works. Although several theories have been offered to explain imagery, none has gained total acceptance. This is neither surprising nor disconcerting—the mechanisms behind many helpful medical procedures, drugs, and psychotherapies are still unclear. Let's briefly summarize four popular explanations for how imagery works in tennis. For more on the theoretical background, see the sources by Ahsen, Lang, Sackett, and White and Hardy in the reference section at the back of the book.

Organized Mental Plan

Some sport psychologists claim that imagery effects are due to enhancing the mental aspects of a task. Thus, imagery helps tennis players prepare strategies, rehearse shot sequences, and improve timing and placement by organizing a mental plan for performance. Although there is research to back this up, some experts believe this is overly simplistic and doesn't fully explain the benefits of imagery.

Content and Physical Response

Another view of imagery holds that an effective image combines items needed for performance—descriptive elements (the feel of the tennis racket, the sight of the ball) and thoughts relevant to the event (such as "this tiebreaker is crucial" or "I have to hold my serve")—with the player's physical reactions to the imagined situation (for example, feeling butterflies during an important point) to reinforce the experience. According to this view, imagery improves performance only when both content and physiological response elements are involved. This perspective of imagery helps explain why smart tennis players are encouraged to build all modes of expression, including thoughts, feelings, actions, and physical sensations, into their images.

Meaning

In addition to the previous view, some experts also believe that the meaning of an image to the person should be included in explaining the wonders of imagery. For example, imagining a long baseline rally before your first state finals tournament would hold a very different meaning to you than imagining your service technique before practice. Thus, benefits occur as a result of imagery content, physical response, and the meaning of the image as well. If you agree with this view, relaxation and deep breathing added to imagery might help you reduce physical sensations of anxiety associated with the great meaning attached to playing in the finals for the first time.

> In the long run the sword is beaten by the mind.
>
> —Napoléon Bonaparte

Improved Psychological State

There is also research that imagery helps the competitor by simulating psychological states such as confidence and attention control. As already stated, imagery will enhance all other mind-body techniques discussed in *Smart Tennis*. Feeling more confident and focused is quite important, and imagery appears to play a huge role in making that happen.

Getting Your Time Machine Ready

We've discussed four possible ways in which imagery might help you perform better as a tennis player. Some day we'll know exactly which of these views is most accurate. Future computer technologies might allow you to load your mental rehearsal sessions onto a virtual reality platform to make them more effective! For the time being, keep relying on your own advanced creative powers and pay attention to the mind-body tools that will make you better.

The following exercises and tips will upgrade your mind-body system for imagery. After you have mastered this section, you're ready to cruise.

Adjusting Your Vision

Since sight is a key sense for imagery, let's begin by adjusting your vision. Athletes often describe imagery from one of two visual perspectives, an internal or external view. Here are these different perspectives:

Internal View

Tennis players using an internal visual perspective imagine themselves inside their own body with the same sensations that they feel in the actual situation. This is a realistic visual perspective because it simulates what you experience on the court. Figure 3.2 depicts what you might imagine with an internal visual perspective.

External View

Those adopting an external visual perspective view themselves from the position of an outside observer or camera perspective. Figure 3.3 illustrates what you might imagine using an external visual perspective.

Figure 3.2
An Internal Visual Imagery Perspective

Figure 3.3
An External Visual Imagery Perspective

Choosing a View

Take a moment to imagine yourself playing in your next tennis match. Put the book down and close your eyes for about thirty seconds. Did you view yourself from an external camera view, or from an internal view as if actually in the match? Although early research seemed to indicate that an internal visual perspective was always preferable to an external one, it's not that simple. Athletes from all sports employ both perspectives while using imagery.

Studies have shown that internal visual imagery is better when performers have to make adjustments in response to changes in what they see, whereas an external perspective is better when performance is judged according to technical form. Both internal and external perspectives are useful in tennis because the sport requires both ongoing adjustment and technical precision. The principles of smart tennis encourage you to use the more realistic internal perspective for most situations, saving the external view for specialized tasks. For imaging long rallies, strategies, or difficult situations, use an internal perspective. You want to make the situation seem as visually realistic as possible. For more simple and controlled situations or movements, an external perspective is appropriate. For example, external imagery can be used to drill specific shots or techniques such as your service, and this visual perspective corresponds well with videotaped pictures. An external perspective is also helpful for imagining repeated setups such as when drilling volleys or overheads. Use imagery from an internal perspective the majority of the time, but use an external perspective occasionally to improve technique.

Tuning in to Your Favorite Channels

Which channels do you enjoy the most? No, I am not referring to selections on your newly purchased digital satellite system. I'm talking about you, a human being with a fully equipped neuroprocessor and six different senses! That's right, six senses—in addition to the five classic senses of sight, hearing, taste, touch, and smell, you also possess the kinesthetic sense that tells you about your body's head and joint positions in space. Since imagery involves programming your mind to use all senses to re-create an experience, it makes sense to scan the system to discover your favorite channels.

Whereas some players are most skillful at re-creating positive visual images, others more naturally visualize physical sensations or sounds. The more vivid you can make your images, the easier it will be to transfer mental rehearsal into actual performance. Although our heads may look similar from the outside, complex brain activity under the skull varies dramatically from one person to the next. Thus everyone experiences their world uniquely! Using imagery only to create pictures when your auditory sense is strongest would be like watching television with poor reception and no sound!

To discover your favorite channels, take a few moments to complete the following exercise, in which we'll be exploring the main senses employed in tennis: sight, sound, and feel. First find a comfortable position in a place where you'll be undisturbed for the next few minutes. After reading over the first image in series one, relax with your eyes closed, breathe deeply and slowly, and create that image in your mind to the best of your ability. Spend about one minute on each image before opening your eyes to read the next image and then repeating the process. After completing all five images in the series, rate how effectively you were able to imagine in that channel by circling a number on a scale of 1 to 10. Higher numbers indicate more skillful use of imagery.

Series One

1. A winter mountain covered partially with pure white snow
2. The red clay tennis courts during the finals of the French Open
3. A yellow tennis ball rising into the air prior to your hitting a smash
4. Your best friend watching you play from the side of the court
5. The image of a tournament draw sheet before your next match

Circle the number indicating your ability to re-create these visual images:

Difficult . . . 1 2 3 4 5 6 7 8 9 10 . . . Easy

Series Two

1. The sounds of clapping and laughter from the crowd
2. The roar of an airplane overhead, getting closer and closer

3. Sounds of the balls hitting rackets at a busy tennis center
4. The rumble of thunder from an approaching storm
5. The sounds of tight racket strings being adjusted from side to side

Circle the number indicating your ability to re-create these sounds:

Difficult . . . 1 2 3 4 5 6 7 8 9 10 . . . Easy

Series Three

1. The feel of sweat running down your face
2. The sensation of a bouncing ball on your racket
3. The way your shoulder muscles ache after a long match
4. The stream of hot water down your back in the shower
5. The feel of a perfectly hit serve

Circle the number indicating your ability to re-create these tactile sensations:

Difficult . . . 1 2 3 4 5 6 7 8 9 10 . . . Easy

Now review which of your three main sensory channels had the best and worst reception. You could also extend this exercise to imagine scenes involving the senses of taste, smell, and head and joint positions in space. Your channel preferences greatly influence how you experience reality. The next time you practice imagery, pay extra attention to the rich variety of sensory experiences in your channel of choice. Later, include even more elaborate detail in that channel to enhance imagery. While on the tennis court, compare your actual sensory experiences with those simulated during imagery. Tune in to your favorite channels both on and off the court and you'll sharpen the quality of your images. Enhance the clarity of images in your least favorite channels too. For example, if you are having difficulty re-creating sounds during imagery, pay greater attention to actual sounds around you. With increased sensory awareness, you'll fine-tune yourself to produce clear and sharp images.

Gain Control Over Your Images

In addition to improving the vividness of images, it's also important to manage your images like a pro. Some players I work with complain that they have difficulty forming their intended images, or that negative or counterproductive images intrude. For example, one player could not visualize himself playing a match without making several unforced errors on easy put-away volleys.

This type of imagery only helps your opponent! Gaining control over your images helps you imagine what you want to accomplish rather than letting bad habits exert a negative influence. The following exercises will help you obtain greater control over your images. By repeating these exercises often, you'll gradually develop improved control over what you are able to imagine.

- *Change a bad habit into a good one:* Consider the worst habit you have as a performer. It may be that you double fault on important points, miss easy volleys, or lose your focus on long rallies. Now close your eyes for a minute or two and imagine that you are performing this skill flawlessly over and over. Make sure your simulated reality is perfect and stay focused throughout.
- *Travel back in time and reverse a loss:* Think back to your most recent disappointing match. It may be an important tournament match against your greatest adversary, or an agonizing recreational loss. Now close your eyes for a few minutes and visualize yourself reversing the outcome by changing your performance. Turn unforced errors into winners, stay positive and focused, and make the changes that would have worked in the match. See yourself performing flawlessly.
- *Travel ahead in time and win the tournament:* Now consider an upcoming tournament or match that you performed poorly in the last time you entered. Close your eyes for a few minutes and imagine the ideal script. See yourself advancing through all rounds to the final.

Imagine yourself with complete poise and confidence, controlled energy, and clear thinking. Everything works according to plan, and you walk off the court the champ.

Now that you've developed a more sensitive mind-body system capable of producing vivid and controllable images from both internal and external perspectives, it's time to examine how to use this tool to make you a better player.

Imagery Guidelines

This section offers you specific guidelines on how to conduct imagery in tennis. These principles are based on the scientific literature and my real-world experience with tennis players.

When to Use Imagery

How much time should you devote to imagery each day? Imagery should become a regular part of your training before, during, and after your matches and practice sessions. Although you are naturally forming images throughout the day when you daydream, the simulated reality produced during imagery is needed to improve your game. Many players consider once a week sufficient for imagery, but they are cheating themselves out of a valuable tool. Would you only engage in physical practice once a week to prepare for an important match? Studies have shown that elite and more successful competitors use imagery more often, and that players at all levels from beginners to world champions benefit if the sessions are conducted properly.

The amount of time devoted to imagery varies depending on your training schedule and goals. A bare minimum is to set aside five minutes before and after each match and practice for mental rehearsal. Thus, if you practice tennis four times a week, you'll spend at least forty minutes per week imaging, not counting on-court imaging. During the match, you are encouraged to use imagery for several seconds before each point and for at least twenty to thirty seconds during changeovers. This may seem like a lot at first, but before long you'll even work imagery into your stretching routine.

What to Imagine

The content of imagery is just as important as knowing which physical skills to practice on the court. Just as you would not improve from practicing with an improper grip, you won't improve by imagining yourself using an improper grip, either. Examine the content of your imagery for accuracy. The old computer saying "garbage in, garbage out" definitely applies here! If your mind-body software is producing flawed images of technique or negative emotional states, it's unlikely that your game will improve. Remember to schedule a lesson with your tennis coach for a technical checkup.

Make sure that you are re-creating all senses in vivid detail during imagery. If you are having trouble with reception in a particular sensory channel, repeat the previous exercises for a greater length of time using even more elaborate images. In addition to creating vivid and controllable images, include the psychological states that you would like to experience on the court as well. For example, imagery should include feelings of confidence, attention control, and proper energy balance. It's worth repeating yet again—you'll use imagery to enhance all the mind-body techniques discussed in *Smart Tennis*. Finally, imagery should be used to re-create specific point sequences and strategies that you would use in the match. The bottom line is that imagery content should be technically precise, clear, vivid, controllable, and realistic in order to produce maximum benefits.

How to Use Imagery

The following techniques will help focus your imagery so that your training is effective and efficient.

Perfect Tennis

Most of the time you should imagine yourself playing flawless but realistic tennis. Create scenarios in which you remain ideally balanced, contact the ball well, and win challenging points. Imaging wild fantasies of hitting scorching winners with your weakest shot will help little. If you are a baseline player with a weak serve, fantasizing yourself playing serve and volley tennis is less useful than a healthy baseline struggle in which you overcome your opponent with consistency. On other occasions, use imagery to develop your game. For example, if you are just learning how to serve and volley, it helps greatly to imagine sequences such as stopping and setting before the opponent makes contact with the ball, or playing your first volley safely into the court. In all cases, however, make sure that your technique and positioning are proper.

Coping with Adversity

A major exception to imaging perfection is called coping imagery. In the spirit of making imagery realistic, you'll occasionally want to overcome a particular problem or negative pattern on the court. It might be a technical flaw or a negative mood state. Allow yourself to imagine the negative situation in vivid detail then immediately follow this sequence with the perfect correction through imagery.

One player with whom I used coping imagery repeatedly became angry and distracted when her opponent played drop shots. She was instructed to imagine an absolutely disastrous point with feelings of anger and poor concentration. She then imagined the same point again, but reversed the images to include sensations of relaxation, control, and clever shot selection to force an error. After identifying her psychological weaknesses in tennis, we repeated this process of traveling back in time to transform negative scenes into more positive ones. Her game eventually improved as she developed confidence, patience, self-control, and remarkable focus.

Be cautious with this form of imagery. Never use imagery in this manner right before a match. Keep negative images to a minimum as you don't want to inadvertently reinforce bad habits!

Time and Motion

Your imagery sessions are more useful if you visualize in real time rather than in slow or fast motion. You may also find it helpful to combine imagery with the same stroking motions and movements involved in actual play. This puts you in touch with your physical sensations and may enhance future images. Remember that your goal is to involve as many modes of human expression as possible, including thoughts, feelings, actions, and physical sensations.

Versions of Imagery

There are as many versions of imagery as there are playing styles, but several work particularly well in tennis.

Long Versions

Imagery can be practiced by lying down in a quiet room, fully relaxed, with eyes closed. This longer version lasts anywhere from fifteen minutes to an hour. Players often use it prior to a match to help prepare them mentally. Here, the idea is to rehearse a perfect performance, often visualizing a complete match point by point. Make sure that you are distraction free, relaxed, and in a comfortable position throughout the session. This longer version works particularly well on the evening before a big match.

Short Versions

A shorter version of imagery, lasting only a few seconds, should be used during the actual match. For example, prior to serving, visualize a perfect serve to the ideal target area, and anticipate the specific sequence of shots that will follow. This is another way that your time machine advances you into the future. Doing this regularly familiarizes you with high-percentage shot sequences, and helps develop anticipation skills for a quicker and more effective response. This version of imagery also works well on changeovers to set in motion a plan for the next game. After developing a basic strategy for the next game, use imagery to rehearse yourself carrying out the plan.

Debriefing Imagery

Following a match, it's useful to spend time conducting a form of imagery that I call debriefing imagery. For the smart tennis player, debriefing imagery is a method of match review with positive reinforcement. Regardless of match outcome, debriefing imagery works the same way every time. Find a quiet place to spend ten minutes imaging everything that you did well in the match. Even if you lost 6–0, 6–0, there are still bright spots to be found. If you won 6–0, 6–0, pick out what you did best and image these aspects of performance. By doing this after every match, you'll reinforce good habits and extinguish bad ones. Since it is based on performance rather than outcome, you'll also reinforce good habits for proper goal setting. (There will be more about goal setting in Chapter Six.)

Prophetic Imagery

Just as it is important to imagine the ideal aspects of a previous performance, it is equally important to put yourself in the right mind-set for a great performance well into the future. Imagery helps here, too. Let's say you are playing in the club championship in one month. Spend nine minutes each night strictly devoted to imagery for this event. For the first three minutes, imagine vivid details of your arrival at the stadium, pre-match routine, and warm-up. Spend the next three minutes vividly imaging the actual match with everything going exactly as planned. Finally, spend the last three minutes after your win. Remember to re-create only positive sensations, thoughts, feelings, and actions, and to use all the mind-body tools you have. If you practice prophetic imagery well in advance of an event, by the time you get there you'll be six steps ahead of your opponent and ready for success.

Specific Tips for Improving Imagery

Here are some specific tips to help you develop better imagery. This section can be used when you are short on time and want to quickly review the important details of exquisite time travel!

- Imagine in vivid detail by re-creating all senses, body awareness, emotions, thoughts, actions, internal sensations, and positive psychological states.
- Only imagine proper technique. If your technique is poor, seek out a qualified tennis professional.
- Use both an internal and external visual perspective with imagery.
- Tune in to your favorite sensory channels during imagery. Elaborate on the details in these

channels while improving the quality of reception in other channels.

- Gain better control over your images by practicing the exercises from this chapter.
- Imagine yourself performing flawlessly unless you are imaging to cope with adversity. In this case, follow the images of adversity with perfect imagery.
- Occasionally use imagery while physically making the same movements you would make playing tennis.
- Use imagery at least five minutes before and after each match and throughout the match.
- Use all forms of imagery, including short and long versions, debriefing imagery, and prophetic imagery.
- Believe that imagery works!

Tennis matches are often decided long before the match in private moments of imagery. Your imagery time machine allows you to access your full range of past experiences while preparing a better future. Players who discover imagery for the first time always wonder how they ever went without it. Enjoy your travels!

Chapter Four introduces the absolutely essential mind-body skill of confidence. Many think that only the most successful champions are confident. However, confident tennis players are never born; they are created by expecting only the best.

4

Confidence

Expecting Only the Best

Vee Kobayashi hadn't done anything physical for nearly forty years. Now—in her late sixties—she had been instructed to get some physical exercise by her cardiac rehabilitation doctor. Encouraged by her husband and her daughter, Vee agreed to try tennis if one of her older friends in the cardiac rehabilitation program would do it with her. She was certain that none of the other patients at the center would be willing. It was a shock to her when her friend Joan volunteered to play with her.

They agreed to start their tennis careers with a semiprivate lesson at a nearby tennis center. As she prepared for the lesson, Vee experienced a mixture of fear and frustration. Fear because she was scared when she thought of making a fool of herself on the court and frustration because she had been physically able to do just about anything she had ever tried as a younger woman. Now, however, she thought she was too old and out of shape to get her body to do what she wanted it to do. To make matters worse, her husband and daughter would be on the sidelines to "cheer" her on. Their presence only made her more nervous and less confident.

The young female instructor asked them about their tennis ability, and taught them the grips. She then asked them to stand at the baseline while she fed balls to their forehand sides. Joan consistently hit the balls back toward the instructor, while Vee was barely able to get her racket near the ball! Her previous doubts and fears came flooding back to her.

The instructor complimented Joan's effort and then proceeded to explain to Vee how to adjust her technique to make good ball contact. Vee started to get annoyed because she understood what to do, she just knew that something was keeping her from doing it. The harder she tried, the more her forehand stroke deteriorated. Vee then became angry at herself. When the lesson ended, the two tennis players decided to try some actual rallying on the court. By this time, Vee was having a tough time controlling her negative self-statements and frustration.

As she walked to the other side of the court, she couldn't even look at her family members sitting patiently at mid court. She was so overwhelmed with frustration and anger that she didn't hear them giving her encouragement. She tried to analyze her feelings. She thought to herself, "How can I expect to hit a tennis ball when I'm this upset?! I either have to control myself or get off this court. Hell, tennis is supposed to be fun. I'm just going to relax, and let whatever happens, happen. If I miss every ball, so what?" Vee let her mind drift back to the lesson, thinking about the instructor's words and her demonstrations.

When both players were ready, Joan hit the ball cleanly over the net. Vee moved to her right, turned, pulled back her racket, and directed it calmly toward the ball. It was startling to her when the ball cruised with good pace back over the net, and right past Joan's swinging racket. Joan and the little audience were startled, too! But not nearly as startled when three of the next four balls hit to her were struck cleanly over the net and into Joan's court. Joan was only able to get to one of them.

Vee lowered her racket and just stared back at Joan. Vee was thrilled, and a smile spread across her face. She realized that the only thing different was her attitude prior to actually returning the balls. It was her negative self-image that was interfering with her ability to make contact during the lesson, nothing else. After this revelation, Vee's confidence improved, she did much better, and she made significant progress over the following weeks in her tennis play.

Vee's fears had kept her from seeing beyond her own limited horizon. When she started to expect success, she began enjoying the sport more and progress followed. Athletes and performers in all endeavors often limit themselves, making damaging assumptions about their abilities and creating barriers to success along the way. Smart tennis players go beyond these silly assumptions by expecting only the best, regardless of past experience, ability, or predicted outcome.

Whether you think you can or think you can't, you are right.
—Henry Ford

Players with an undeveloped mind-body skill of confidence are all too aware of their place in the competitive hierarchy, and take a back seat to those they perceive as better at the game. Although it's natural to acknowledge and appreciate talent in others, remember that even the world's best put on their pants one leg at a time. Not being overly impressed by the opponent helps build an attitude that is second to none. Smart tennis players are never limited by the horizon. They look way beyond the horizon, gain a brighter outlook, and return with confidence to realize better performance.

I've always emphasized confidence as a key foundation from which many other mind-body skills flow. With confidence in place anything is possible, but without it you might as well stay home and watch someone else perform. One player I recently worked with described her growth in this area:

I used to let my fears get the best of me, and my confidence depended upon my previous match results. I'm beginning to realize that confidence is something that only I control, and with it I am calmer, more focused, and excited about possibilities that I would not have considered before. I definitely perform better.

As with all mind-body skills, confidence for this player was apparent in her thoughts (control), emotions (less fear), physical sensations (calmer), and actions (perform better). She learned that confidence is available to anyone who practices it. Sometimes it appears that only the most elite athletes have access to that magical confidence, while all other inferior beings can only wish for it. Fortunately, this is wrong! You can increase your level of confidence. Winning is never guaranteed, but expectations of success are always possible and enhance your chances to perform better.

Introducing Confidence

Athletes have long recognized a positive relationship between confidence and performance. Confidence is defined as "the belief that you can perform a desired behavior," but for the smart tennis player it is much more than that. It's really an umbrella term that describes all the thoughts, feelings, actions, and physical sensations reflecting self-belief and expectations of success. Confident athletes entertain a rich variety of successful thoughts. The thought of failure rarely occurs. Confident athletes believe deeply in their abilities, love challenges, and feel strongly that they will prevail. Finally, confident athletes expect success and display it in their body language. They rarely give their opponent a confidence boost by appearing discouraged or threatened.

No man (or woman) can make you feel inferior without your consent.
—Eleanor Roosevelt

Take a moment to reflect on some of your most recent performances. Did thoughts or feelings of failure ever intrude? If so, you will be glad to acquire and hone this mind-body skill. Although negative states can occur in any performance situation, the goal is to minimize these as much as possible and replace them with high expectations. Just like unforced errors, thoughts and feelings of failure have the cumulative effect of destroying your game.

I'm often asked what comes first, confidence or success? Although it is true that success is contagious and breeds confidence, it is equally true that confidence increases one's probability for success. Success is never certain, but self-doubt, negativity, and low expectations guarantee failure. Belief in oneself prevents harmful distractions such as anxiety, allowing for a more efficient performance focus. Confidence also adds security during slumps and helps the athlete sustain effort. Finally, self-belief prompts athletes to set higher performance goals, as greater achievements are expected and appear more attainable. Those who lack confidence worry needlessly about mistakes, lose concentration, allow dangerous levels of arousal to intrude, and hasten failure by giving up. After all, it seems to someone in that state of mind, there is nothing to gain by trying.

No Substitute for Skill

Players sometimes ask if improving their confidence will make them an overnight success. My answer is not unless this is the only piece you are missing in your game. Although confidence is desired by all, there is no replacement for proper technique, hard work, and smart practice. The most confident performers in the world still need skill and experience to succeed, but confidence makes everything go more smoothly and often spells the difference in outcome. As a mind-body tool that has a most widespread positive effect, there is just no substitute for confidence!

Overconfidence

Can too much confidence be bad? Absolutely! As with most things, the key to confidence is moderation. What does it mean to be overconfident or cocky? Many describe the relationship between confidence and performance as an inverted U, such that gains in confidence will help you up to a point, after which too much confidence is dangerous. Maintaining an optimal level of confidence is important. Overconfidence, or a false belief in one's ability, can lead to reduced effort and performance. So while it's important to believe fully in your chances for success, it's also important to maintain a healthy dose of modesty, knowing that without a complete effort performance will suffer. Figure 4.1 depicts the inverted U relationship between confidence and performance.

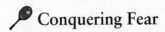

Conquering Fear

After you've looked far beyond the limited horizons of others and recognized the power of self-belief, there's still a nasty beast to battle before confidence can express itself. Its name is *fear*—and it can be a truly terrifying emotion in tennis. Fear is healthy in truly fearful situations. It's good to be afraid of danger, and to avoid it. But here, I'm talking about fear in tennis. Do you remember the last time you were struck by fear in a match?

Figure 4.1
The Relationship Between Confidence and Performance

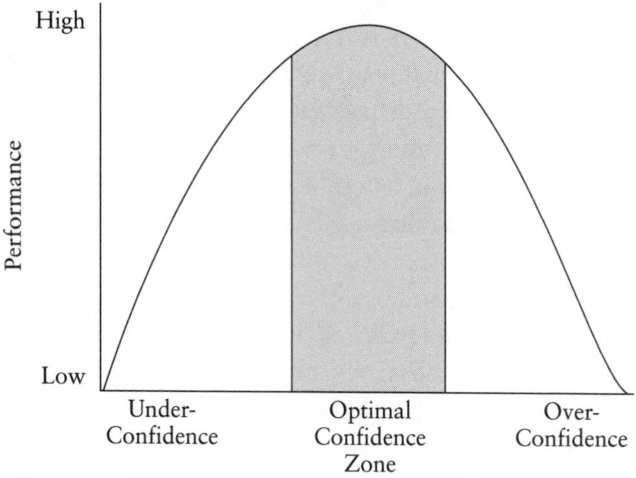

If it threw off your performance on a decisive point, you have plenty of company! Let's identify, confront, and destroy this feisty foe.

Identify the Monster

In my work with elite athletes trying to achieve extraordinary results and with clients just trying to adapt to everyday stress, themes of fear and anxiety come up quite often. People go to great lengths to avoid their objects of fear—but this only leads to greater fear.

Avoidance of the feared object or situation feeds fear like oxygen feeds fire. Just as monsters in the dark are eliminated by switching on the lights, conquering fear requires an openness to face the source of fear. Figure 4.2 shows what happens when you face your fears.

My dictionary defines *fear* as a distressing emotion aroused by impending pain, danger, or evil, whether real or imagined. In tennis, fear is usually elicited by the possibility of making a mistake, appearing incompetent, or losing. Other descriptions of fear are self-doubt, worry, concern, and negative thoughts or feelings.

Fear may lead to negative outcomes including dangerously high arousal, impaired concentration, tensed muscles, lost rhythm, indecision, expectations of failure, and lowered perceptions of control. Although this emotion effectively warned our ancestors of approaching predators in the wild, the most threatening predator on the tennis court is often fear itself!

Typically, fear increases with the perceived importance of the situation. Play becomes more conscious, careful, and tentative in an attempt to avoid mistakes. The term *choking* is used to describe this effect. A serve that was once loose and fluid turns into a fat marshmallow, and groundstrokes are awkwardly steered and pushed for added security. Opponents not overcome by these same tendencies quickly realize an opportunity, play more aggressively, and assume control of the match.

Figure 4.2
Confronting Your Fears Head On

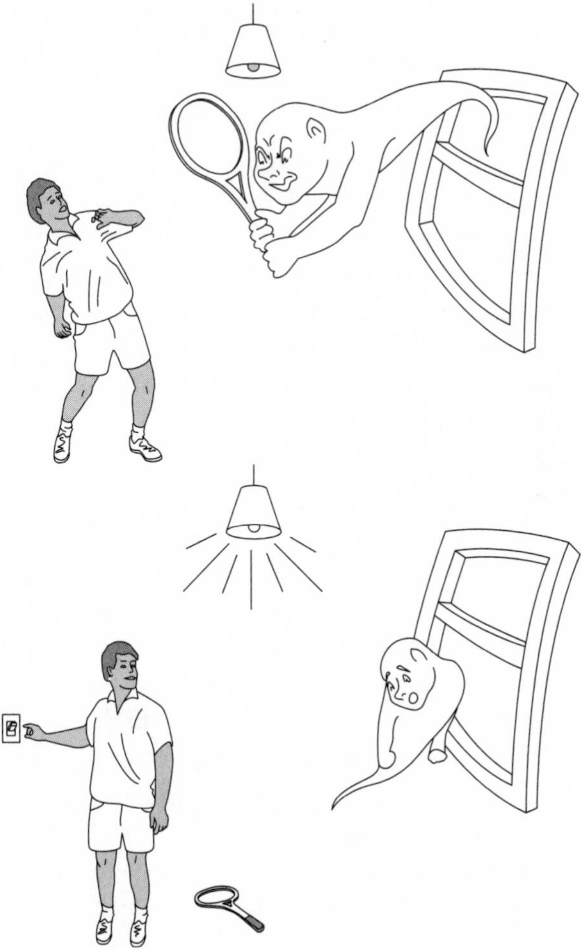

It is important to distinguish between fear and nervousness. Whereas fear is always a negative mental state, nervousness is a physical condition (shown in increased heart rate, sweating, and so on) that can actually improve play. Martina Navratilova admitted that she always got nervous playing tennis and had to gradually learn that it was not a weakness. Jack Nicklaus stated that he did not know how to play great golf when he was not nervous. So while nervousness provides a great source of energy to enhance performance in critical moments, fearful thinking about what might go wrong is a useless menace.

Steps to Eliminate Fear

Now that we've identified the beast of fear, let's look at some ways to clear the path to greater confidence. Begin by recognizing that there are no quick or easy solutions guaranteed to eliminate fear from your game. Since fear arises as a result of your own appraisals and expectations, it will be important to comprehend performance in a slightly different way. Just as disregarding your opponent's greatness helps build self-belief, start forgetting how others might see you. Your perceptions about yourself are most important. Begin thinking like a winner both on and off the court. Frequently imagine what you would like to have happen while avoiding doubtful thinking about possible misfortunes. Keep an active memory of times when you performed well and learn to eliminate memories of bad performances.

When struck by fear during a match, realize that your opponent probably feels the same way or worse. Focus concretely on what you are going to accomplish and then just do it. Practice beginning matches at 15–40, 4–5 in the final set. Learn to love this challenge. Maintain an aggressive style of play rather than becoming tentative. Your best tennis comes when you are relaxed, poised, and full of belief in your abilities. You cannot control the outcome and you cannot always win, but by confronting your fears head on you'll develop greater confidence.

It is useless to fear losing since we are only able to control our own performance. Minimizing fear calms us down and helps us play better. This improved performance leads to even higher confidence. Players who play smart tennis have no use for fear because they place their value on the next point rather than the possibility of losing. The only true fear in tennis is not doing your very best on the next point, and this fear is unnecessary too because there is another point just around the corner!

Becoming Your Own Master

With a richer sense of self-belief, and fear without a leg to stand on, it's time to take further action to develop the mind-body skill of confidence. In addition to expanding your horizon and eliminating fear, you'll want to start developing a true sense of mastery in everything you do. Why let someone else be your master when you have every right to become your own master?

A theme evident throughout this book is the importance of investing in self-knowledge. The Tennis Mind-Body Checklist in Chapter One is a great starting point to gain valuable information about your thoughts, feelings, actions, and physical sensations across the five mind-body skill areas. As you go through the checklist again from time to time, you'll further increase your awareness of those areas needing improvement. Unfortunately, knowledge alone is rarely sufficient. Having an additional sense of mastery—of perceived competence in your ability to perform and improve—greatly enhances your confidence as well as your chances for success. This requires that you first explore your current skill level and find ways to steadily improve.

Determining Your Skill Level

What is your current skill level in tennis? Some players rate themselves on a three-level scale (Beginner, Intermediate, Advanced), while others use the seven-point scale derived by the National Tennis Rating Program (NTRP). Exhibit 4.1 provides a condensed version of the NTRP scale.

Exhibit 4.1
The National Tennis Rating Program Scale

Rating	*Description*
1.0	Just starting to play tennis.
1.5	Has limited experience and is still working primarily on getting the ball into play.
2.0	Needs on-court experience. Has obvious stroke weaknesses but is familiar with basic positions for singles and doubles play.
2.5	Learning to judge where the ball is going although court coverage is weak. Can sustain a short rally of slow pace with other players of the same ability.
3.0	Fairly consistent when hitting medium-paced shots, but not comfortable with all strokes and lacks execution when trying for directional control, depth, or power. Most common doubles formation is one-up and one-back.
3.5	Has achieved improved stroke dependability with directional control on moderate shots, but still lacks depth and variety. Exhibits more aggressive net play, has improved court coverage and is developing teamwork in doubles.
4.0	Has dependable strokes, including directional control and depth on both forehand and backhand sides on moderate shots, plus the ability to use lobs, overheads, approach shots and volleys with some success. Occasionally forces errors when serving. Rallies may be lost due to impatience. Teamwork in doubles is evident.
4.5	Starting to master the use of power and spins and beginning to handle pace, has sound footwork, can control depth on shots and is beginning to vary game plan according to opponents. Can hit first serves with power and accuracy and place the second serve.

(cont'd.)

(cont'd.)

	Tends to overhit on difficult shots. Aggressive net play is common in doubles.
5.0	Has good shot anticipation and frequently has an outstanding shot around which a game may be structured. Can regularly hit winners or force errors off short balls and can put away volleys, can successfully execute lobs, drop shots, half volleys and overhead smashes and has good depth and spin on most second serves.
5.5	Has developed power or consistency (or both) as a major weapon. Can vary strategies and styles of play in a competitive situation and hit dependable shots in a stress situation.
6.0	Has had intensive training for national tournament competition at the junior and collegiate levels and has obtained a sectional and/or national ranking.
6.5	Has extensive satellite tournament experience.
7.0	A world class player committed to tournament tennis on the international level and whose major source of income is tournament prize winnings.

Source: United States Tennis Association. Reprinted by permission.

Whether you use a traditional rating system or not, there are probably more like a thousand different skill levels in tennis. So, while a beginner might love to climb from level 21 to 22, Pete Sampras and Marcello Rios are likely shooting for level 997. A thousand levels puts things in perspective, but even Sampras would never trick himself into believing he had "arrived." Such an attitude might only sabotage his next performance as a result of overconfidence.

Meaningful Improvement

Meaningful improvement and increased confidence come from learning new techniques that are adaptive in competition—and then applying them consistently. Your progress can be seen in many ways, such as winning for the first time against a frequent opponent, advancing further in tournaments, or improving your ranking. Your focus should be directed mostly on performance rather than on match outcome, however, since thoughts of winning and losing are irrelevant distractions. (We'll talk more about this in Chapter Six on goal setting.) Keep in mind that outcomes are determined by the relative contributions of each competitor, so don't gloat too long after a win or become too upset following a loss. Your peak performance might occur during an agonizing loss, and your most hideous production ever could win you prize money! Take a breath, step back, and look at improvement as a never-ending and exciting journey.

Perceived Competence

Regardless of your actual performance level, rating, or ranking, how competent and effective do you feel as a player? Take a moment to consider how this attitude of mastery varies across different situations and against different opponents. There is much research and experience to support the value of a strong sense of mastery in meeting challenges. Seeing yourself as competent and effective in tennis might even extend benefits far beyond the sport. A perceived sense of mastery, or feeling of control, has been shown to generalize to many other areas including stress reactions, achievement strivings, career pursuits, and even health and survival!

How do you increase your sense of mastery and gain even more confidence? Here are four tips to guide you in developing an approach to problems:

- Explain poor performance and negative events as being within rather than outside your control.
- Take full responsibility for the changes you desire. Believe that your efforts, work habits, and self-discipline will lead to improvement.
- Performance accomplishments naturally lead to a higher sense of mastery. To accelerate learning, frequently watch experts, visualize their performances, and solicit feedback from them about your own technique.
- Interpret increases in arousal as energy for performance rather than as stress, anxiety, or fear. (In Chapter Five we'll learn more about energy control for enhanced play.)

With a greater sense of mastery and primary focus on performance rather than outcome, you will be more in the driver's seat than ever. Confidence and skill level go hand in hand. Whether you slowly climb the ladder of a thousand levels or break the top fifty in the world for the first time, your confidence will probably rise too.

As your skills and confidence rise, it's natural to experience minor setbacks in your performance—progress never follows a direct, linear path. It's quite normal to have dips in performance as you are beginning to integrate new mind-body skills into your game. When this happens, remember that only you can control your confidence level. Although you may take a step or two back every so often, you'll take three or four steps forward again soon. Expect minor setbacks and view your progress as an upwardly moving spiral. This will help you keep your head up when the going gets a little rough, as it often will.

Figure 4.3 depicts the rise and fall of performance over time. Notice that over the long run, performance continues to improve.

The Comfort Trap

You've already been introduced to ways of conquering fear to obtain greater confidence. An equally dangerous mental state often arises in the absence of fear, when you're in total command of the match and on the verge of victory. This state is called *the comfort trap* and it's a form of overconfidence that can demoralize its victims. Let's prevent the comfort trap from destroying your confidence and performance.

Figure 4.3
The Progress Spiral

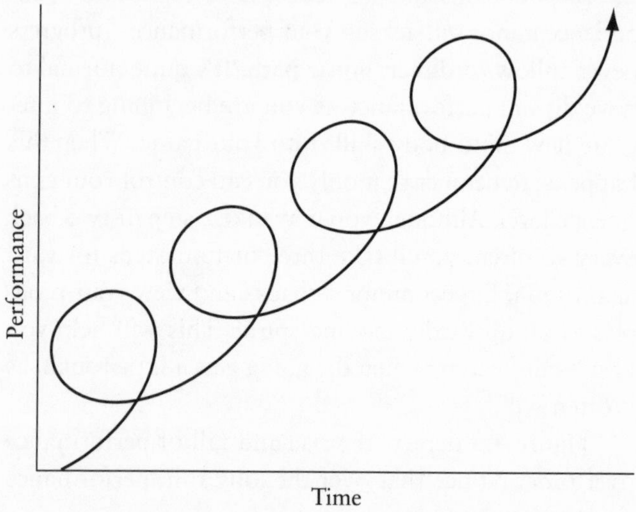

Illusion Followed by Agony

Many competitors fail to realize that being close to an easy victory is actually one of the most vulnerable situations in the game. There is little additional perceived gain in winning because winning just meets your expectations for the match. On the other hand, losing can appear quite traumatic because it is far below expectations. Ever so slight self-satisfaction on the part of the leader combined with the gritty determination of a wounded opponent can turn the match around dramatically. If negative thoughts, fears of choking, and reduced confidence intrude, expect a major turnaround.

Players at all levels have experienced the agony and frustration of failing to put the match away. One example was Jana Novotna's 1993 Wimbledon finals vanishing act after being up 4–1, 40–30 in the final set against Steffi Graf. Applaud Graf's comeback, but Novotna was scratching her head until her 1998 triumph on the grass! With a big lead, it's important to know how to win.

The Killer Instinct

To stay out of the all-too-dangerous comfort trap, remind yourself that the match isn't over until the final point, and that the opponent often plays best when there is nothing left to lose. The ability to close out the match is called the *killer instinct* and it's the best remedy for the comfort trap. However, the killer instinct is not really an instinct at all! It needs to be understood, practiced, and refined over and over just like all mind-body skills.

Let's take a moment to consider what's needed to develop and maintain the killer instinct in tennis. Here are a few tips:

- Never become comfortable with a lead, as there are no guarantees for victory. Games are often won and lost in streaks, so always be wary of your opponent's ability to rally. Stay focused on performance rather than outcome.

- With a commanding lead, play games with yourself to avoid a letdown. Pretend that you are really several games behind and need a complete effort just to remain in the match.
- Decreased arousal often accompanies a letdown. If you find your energy level slipping or note that you're beginning to lose interest in the match, fire yourself back up to an optimal arousal level. (We'll talk more about how to do this in the next chapter.)
- Overconfidence is a major trap leading to reduced effort and performance. Find the right mixture of poise and modesty.
- Avoid thinking about or discussing the final score or your next opponent. Stay completely focused on the present and eliminate all other distractions. (If you need a refresher on how to do this, refer back to Chapter Two on attention control.)
- Keep the pressure on your opponent by playing well with a big lead rather than just doing what it takes to win. Your goal should be to convince your opponents that they have absolutely no chance of a comeback.

It takes practice to consistently close out matches that should be won. Don't wait for your opponent's next dramatic comeback to realize this truth. If your opponent does happen to sneak back and win after being far behind, keep the progress spiral in mind and stay positive. Keep working on the killer instinct and just realize that your own chance to pull off a major comeback is just around the corner.

Social Support and Positive Thinking

Performing your absolute best is no easy task. Success in any endeavor is often accompanied by large doses of stress, setbacks, and adversity, and confidence is sometimes difficult to maintain despite all the self-knowledge and practice in the world. It's hard to imagine coping with everything alone, but tennis is an individual sport and many tennis players try to survive on their own wits without seeking the support of others. In the course of my international tennis coaching career, I have noticed that tennis players in the United States appeared to rely less on the support of others than in many other countries, where family and group factors are more emphasized. It is my opinion that these lonely warriors often missed out on a great positive influence. Self-belief must always come from within and independence is a virtue—but gaining the support of others is valuable too!

How Others Can Help

Social support feeds confidence and makes the game more enjoyable, less stressful—and more prosperous. No performer is an island. Having social support means being involved in relationships, connected with other people, and feeling understood and cared for. Two forms of social support are caring and emotional support, and help and guidance. Whereas the first type provides the athlete a valuable sense of being understood and appreciated, the second offers specific information and direction needed to thrive in a competitive setting.

A sampling of the research shows that social support reduces stress, lowers the incidence of health-threatening behavior and illness, increases perception of control, and lengthens life span. Results from my Ph.D. dissertation at the University of Florida showed that perceptions of social support coincided with more positive mood states among members of the 1996 national champion Florida Gators football team. Whether social support was a major factor in helping Florida win the national title is difficult to say, but social support among these top-level athletes was much higher than among a matched group of recreational athletes. Although they need social support as much as anyone, tennis players often lack the large social support resources found in team sports. Whether at the recreational or elite level, this may leave them particularly vulnerable to stress when the going gets rough.

Enhancing Support

Many tennis players consider it a sign of weakness to seek out help, isolating themselves when distressed.

Experience and scientific wisdom indicate that "a little help from your friends" is a much better solution.

Here are some ways to enhance social support:

- Share your problems and goals with your friends, colleagues, and teammates. Rather than being criticized for your openness, you'll probably find that your efforts to disclose aspects of yourself are very well received. If an issue is too sensitive, share it only with those closest to you, or seek professional counseling.
- Offer social support to others when they need it. The listening and sincerity you provide will be amply reciprocated when it's your turn to need support.
- Seek out a support group away from your sport. Alternative social networks provide great balance in life, giving you a boost similar to the effects of cross-training for physical fitness.

We're all in this great game together and relying upon one another for support is both fun and wise. Don't neglect this powerful source of positive thinking, confidence, and improved performance.

Keeping a Healthy Tennis Perspective

Few individuals thrive on negativity or pressure. The key is to remove pressure with healthy, positive thoughts.

Keep in mind that tennis is just a sport and that sports should be fun, rewarding, challenging, and growth enhancing. I've identified fourteen tips or pointers that can help you keep tennis in a healthy perspective. With these fourteen confidence-building principles in hand, you'll be ready to hunt even the largest tigers with renewed enthusiasm and move further down the road toward personal fulfillment.

1. *Don't get too serious:* Give your absolute best, but reinterpret a loss as simply an excellent lesson for the next match.
2. *Have fun:* Enjoyment helps you learn faster and perform better.
3. *Never give up:* Even when down 6–0, 5–0, the match is not yet over. Staying positive in these situations reinforces the values of consistency and perseverance, and builds confidence.
4. *Believe in yourself:* On and off the court, self-belief improves performance and builds character.
5. *Imagine successful performances:* Use imagery frequently, invoking as many senses as possible to enhance the experience. You might like to review Chapter Three on imagery and develop a long-term memory for those things that you do well.

6. *Increase your physical fitness:* This will enhance your technique and your self-image at the same time! There are few better way to expect success than to enjoy the feeling and knowledge that your body is prepared and ready.
7. *Play weaker opponents on occasion:* You need some victories to keep your confidence alive. Some players never learn to win or develop confidence because they are always overmatched. There is nothing wrong with playing down occasionally—and your opponent will appreciate the chance to play up.
8. *List your mental and physical strengths:* Make it a long list! If this is difficult, ask someone to help you. Review your list regularly to remind yourself how great you really are. Many players recall the negative readily while ignoring the obvious good right in front of them.
9. *Eliminate negative thoughts:* When they do occur, replace them with positive self-statements such as, "I'm at my best under pressure." Frequently think of positive self-statements during imagery, and replace any negative memories that crop up with positive ones.
10. *Develop primary and secondary competitive strategies:* Have a strategy going into each

competition and a backup strategy ready to go in case your main plan fails. Scout your opponent if possible before the match and line up your strengths against your opponent's weaknesses. Confidence will grow as you execute your plan.

11. *Maintain positive body language:* Keep your head up regardless of the score. The way you act will influence the way you and your opponent think and feel. Act confident, be confident!
12. *Practice improving your weaknesses:* Use your practice time to give you more to believe in during competition. Remember that practice does not make perfect. Only perfect practice makes perfect. Work hard in the previews and the main events will be more fun.
13. *Don't idolize opponents:* Although you need a healthy respect for each opponent so as to guard against overconfidence, realize that barriers to success and confidence are often self-imposed. It's easy to give your adversary too much credit. Instead, focus on your own strengths and performance.
14. *Love tough challenges:* The best way to improve confidence is to prepare well, go for it with all your heart and mind, and allow the

outcome to take care of itself. By learning to enjoy competition, you are making yourself a better player and building confidence too.

Exhibit 4.2 summarizes these fourteen confidence-building principles for quick review.

Exhibit 4.2
Principles That Develop Confidence in Tennis

1. Don't get too serious.
2. Have fun.
3. Never give up.
4. Believe in yourself.
5. Imagine successful performances.
6. Increase your physical fitness.
7. Play weaker opponents on occasion.
8. List your mental and physical strengths.
9. Eliminate negative thoughts.
10. Develop primary and secondary competitive strategies.
11. Maintain positive body language.
12. Practice improving your weaknesses.
13. Don't idolize opponents.
14. Love tough challenges.

Although it may appear that confidence is an inborn trait only reserved for the noble and gifted, there is nothing further from the truth. Confidence is attainable by all and should be practiced and refined like any other mind-body skill. Confidence is a habit of highly successful performers, and you have the ability to control it 100 percent. Remove your limited horizon, believe in yourself, and prosper!

In the next chapter we'll discover the right balance of power through energy control. Energy control optimizes your arousal level and keeps you charged for continued success.

5

Energy Control
The Right Balance of Power

Tamara Morgan considered herself assertive. It was something she was quite proud of in her job as a supervisor in one of the offices of the Miami Department of Motor Vehicles. If there was a job to get done, she took it on. If there was a customer that one of her subordinates needed help with, she found the time to listen, evaluate, and provide guidance to solve public relations problems. She actually enjoyed problems and loved to dig right into them. When she did, she poured her entire heart and soul into their solution. And that's the way she played tennis.

Tammy was first introduced to the sport in a college tennis course. She played for two years after college, seemed to improve every week, and found a lot of satisfaction in learning tennis skills. Then she tried a couple of singles tournaments. She surprised herself a little by actually winning the first one, a local country club event at the 3.0 level. This really pumped her up. But that was the last tournament that she ever won. In fact, in the three more tournaments that she entered, she never got past the second round. In all three of those events, she'd found herself rushing her shots, sailing balls well over the baseline, and smashing overheads into the net. That was not the way she usually played. There was something different about tournament play that she just couldn't quite understand. It seemed like everything was happening too fast for her in those tournaments. She found the experience so dissatisfying that she lost interest in tennis and quit playing.

Years later, in search of some physical exercise, Tammy enrolled in a tennis class. The instructor was Mark Jensen, a Miami junior college physical education teacher who had studied sport psychology at San Diego State University before moving to Miami. Mark told her that she seemed "over activated" when she played in the course's end-of-semester tournament. Mark's choice of words really hit a chord with Tammy. That was exactly the way she'd felt in those tournaments years earlier.

Mark suggested that she'd probably been overaroused in those tournaments, just the way she appeared to be in the class tournament. When she seemed genuinely interested in learning more about arousal and tennis, Mark took some time with her to explain the relationship between performance and energy control. It was as if a light went on in Tammy's head. She finally understood why she'd played so poorly in those early tournaments. "You know, it's too bad I didn't know about this long ago," she said. "Well, you know about it now," Mark answered. "Why don't you see if you can put it into practice?" He explained about senior tournaments, pointing out that older players can still find healthy competition in tournament play, and it was only a matter of time before Tammy asked him if he would help her learn to control her energy level in another tournament.

A week before Tammy's first tennis tournament in over a decade, Mark introduced a technique called *stress inoculation.* In the middle of a practice rally, he caught the ball and threw it to her, saying, "Serve." She nodded, took the ball, and began bouncing it in preparation for serving.

"OK, lady," Mark announced. "This is the finals. There are three hundred people watching this match. Your husband and children are courtside. The newspaper reporters are here, and, look at that, a TV crew is just setting up their cameras, too.

"You've lost the first set, and you're tied at 4 all in the second. You're down a break point and have just missed your first serve. If you double fault, your opponent takes a 5–4 lead and will be serving. This is a critically important serve. If you hit it too soft, you know that your opponent is going to jump on it. As you bounce the ball prior to this second serve, you keep getting images of serving the ball into the net. What are you going to do?"

As Mark described the scenario to her, Tammy felt herself becoming nervous. It wasn't an unpleasant sensation—over the past two months Mark had helped her see that some nervousness in competition is natural and in the right amounts can actually be motivating. But as he continued adding stressors, Tammy could feel herself going beyond nervousness into overarousal. She'd learned from Mark that in such cases her performance would plummet. She knew she had to bring her level of energy back under control.

She quickly checked her body for excess muscular tension and realized that her shoulders and neck felt tight. She purposefully contracted the muscles in her neck, shoulders, and upper back; then let them go. As she did, she said a "mood" word that she and Mark had agreed to: "*calm.*" She then took two slow breaths and said a positive affirmation about her serving ability. "You are an excellent second server, Tamara." Next, she focused on her opponent's position and objectively decided where she would place her service. Finally, resuming her ball bounces, she reminded herself to toss high, and to make good solid contact. "This is just like practice with Mark," she said to herself as she made a perfect toss, and hit a solid serve past her instructor.

Mark made no attempt to return the serve. He just stood there with his arms crossed and a smile on his face. "Progressive muscle relaxation, easy breathing, a positive self-statement, and centering on the task at hand?" he asked. "Uh huh!" she nodded as she walked to the net. "You'll be ready next week," he said, still smiling.

Tammy's newly discovered confidence and consistency would never have been possible if she hadn't learned to regulate energy. Energy is needed for any performance. Whether nuclear energy in a submarine, gasoline in your car, or just being mentally and physically charged for your best tennis ever, energy is essential. Elite athletes are always looking for better energy control. Studies in psychology and the sport sciences devote tremendous attention to this topic. This chapter combines the latest scientific wisdom with years of experience to help you find the right energy balance for optimal performance.

Many factors influence energy levels—desire, stress, anxiety, fatigue, and excitement, to name just a few. Energy levels, in turn, affect your ability to perform efficiently; they can lead to outcomes ranging from choking (discussed in Chapter Two) to peak performance.

I've seen the influence of energy control in every performer I've ever worked with. One tennis player described his difficulty controlling his energy before important matches:

Before the match, I'm so high-strung that by the warm-up I'm completely wiped out, both mentally and physically. This leads to negative thinking as I lose my focus, play recklessly, and then just cash in my chips.

The damage inflicted by poor energy control was evident in this player's thoughts (negative), feelings (high-strung), actions (reckless play, giving up) and physical sensations (fatigue). He was a challenge to work with, but by changing his views about competition and learning to relax more effectively, he assumed greater control over his energy levels. He was still sometimes nervous and uptight before important matches, but he learned to lower his physical arousal before the match began. Performance began to improve once negative thoughts and anxiety were eliminated.

His unflagging energy explodes into virtually every muscular topspinning shot, with sound effects that make Monica Seles seem mute.

—Bud Collins,
on Thomas Muster

Although excessively high levels of negative energy impair performance, low energy levels can be just as much a problem. Let's examine energy more closely. *Energy* is the term used in the smart tennis approach, but other words that have been similarly used include *arousal, activation,* and *intensity.*

Energy Defined

Despite Einstein's widely accepted theory of relativity, definitions of energy and its effect on performance in sport are still hotly debated. Fine distinctions are made between various energy states, and there seem to be as many disagreements as there are agreements! In my opinion, this reflects the diversity of performance demands across sports, which vary on a continuum from sinking a two-foot putt to putting away a decisive smash for the match to landing a crushing blow on the fullback. Add to these task differences the multiple skill levels and personalities of the performers and the whole picture can seem quite intimidating! Our focus on optimizing energy levels *in tennis* makes this job much easier.

Energy for the smart tennis player is an arousing agent of the mind and body. The overall effects of different energy levels vary widely—from deep sleep to extreme excitement. In addition, energy is directed into each of the four mind-body dimensions separately. For example, energy influences physical sensations (such as increasing your heart rate), thoughts (such as focusing more intensely on an event), emotions (such as irritability or excitement), and actions (such as running faster). Another way to view energy is as a motivational state that directs one toward a specific goal.

Anxiety and Stress

Energy should be distinguished from anxiety and stress. Although anxiety usually leads to increases in energy or arousal, it is also accompanied by worry, concern, or other negative thoughts and feelings. Stress, on the other hand, is a state in which a demand is made on a person and the person is required to cope with the demand. Stress has also been described as stimulation that grossly disturbs homeostasis or stability. So, whereas anxiety and stress are usually viewed negatively, energy levels may be more or less appropriate depending on the nature of the task, situation, and person.

Seven Energy Sources

In searching for the fabled fountain of youth, the explorer Ponce de Leon never found the energy he desired—but then, he never read this chapter! Having defined energy and distinguished it from anxiety and stress, let's look at some of the best ways of acquiring this mind-body fuel. You may be surprised at how abundant it really is. Here are my seven favorite sources of energy.

Active Moods

Your moods vary from day to day and moment to moment, but represent a solid source of energy. Whenever you are feeling angry, tense, or lively, these active moods can be tapped and converted into positive energy for tennis. Less active moods such as dejection and fatigue deplete energy sources, but steps can be taken to alter these moods to increase energy. For example, distracting yourself from fatigue through proper attention control increases your energy supply. For a review of attention control, refer to Chapter Two.

Determination

Sheer willpower is a great personal source of energy. Just knowing that you'll give it your all and never resign, regardless of the situation, helps a lot. One way to keep this resource abundant is to set meaningful performance goals before each match. When we get to Chapter Six on goal setting, you'll learn more about meaningful performance.

Competitive Excitement

Competition, with its uncertainty, pleasure, and excitement, often generates abundant energy. Keep this fuel around by having fun, smiling, and loving the healthy struggle you encounter as a performer.

Physical Well-Being

Staying physically fit, well-nourished, and rested provides you an extra energy advantage that will carry you through even the most grueling performances. Competition is much more efficient and enjoyable when you are physically prepared.

Social Influences

The energy boost provided by others can be significant. Positive social support is a great resource, but casual onlookers and even nasty opponents can serve to increase your energy levels. *Social facilitation* is the term describing the effect in which performance improves in front of an audience. This audience effect works best with simple skills or more advanced performers. If you're a beginner, develop your skills and confidence first without an audience present. If you're advanced, by all means invite the whole city to your performances!

Confidence and Self-Esteem

Expecting success and valuing yourself highly are two of the most powerful sources of energy available. There are few substitutes for confidence, which we discussed extensively in Chapter Four. Keep in mind that this resource is available to players at every level—even beginners can adjust their mind-set to expect success!

Take care of yourself and your energy resources will remain high.

Imagery and Self-Talk

As we discussed in Chapter Three, proper imagery can deliver powerful amounts of energy. Combined with positive self-statements, these tools create positive fuel for a smart tennis game.

Energy-Performance Relationship

Now that we have plenty of ways to acquire energy, let's see how it's linked with performance.

Four-Cylinder Efficiency

There have been many descriptions of the relationship between energy and performance. More energy is not always better. Energy manifests across all dimensions, so increases in one area combined with decreases in another often produce best results. For example, you might jump up and down a few times between points to increase your heart rate, yet still try to maintain less intense, calmer, and more relaxed thoughts and feelings. Although you might need to fire yourself up physically, also intensifying your thinking could lead to worry, narrowed attention (which we explored in Chapter Two), and impaired performance. The key, as always, is to find the right energy balance.

Controlling energy levels is like adjusting the firing rate in each piston of a four-cylinder engine. You get great fuel efficiency with four cylinders, and each piston represents a different mind-body dimension. This balanced, efficient energy system is illustrated in Figure 5.1.

Keeping your mind-body system running smoothly requires that you understand the competitive situation and the right amount of energy needed from each dimension at the right time. Mastering this skill takes self-awareness and lots of practice, but just think how lost your opponents will be if they aren't even considering energy balance.

Let's turn our attention to some classic views of the energy-performance relationship. Keep in mind that smart tennis players ultimately mix their own mind-body fuel for success.

Figure 5.1
Four-Cylinder Energy Efficiency

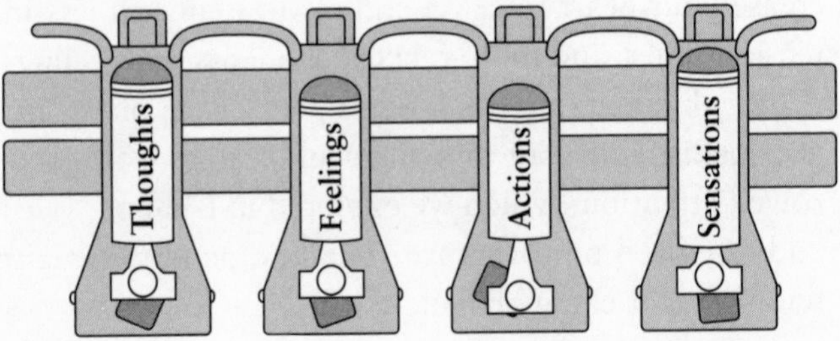

The Inverted U

One of the oldest psychological theories describing the relationship between arousal and performance is the "Inverted-U Hypothesis." This theory states that optimal performance is achieved with increases in physiological arousal until further increases lead to performance decreases. When graphed visually, the resulting pattern resembles an inverted U shape as illustrated in Figure 5.2.

Sport psychologists also describe "zones of optimal functioning," reflecting the idea that it's impossible to

Figure 5.2
The Energy-Performance Relationship in Tennis

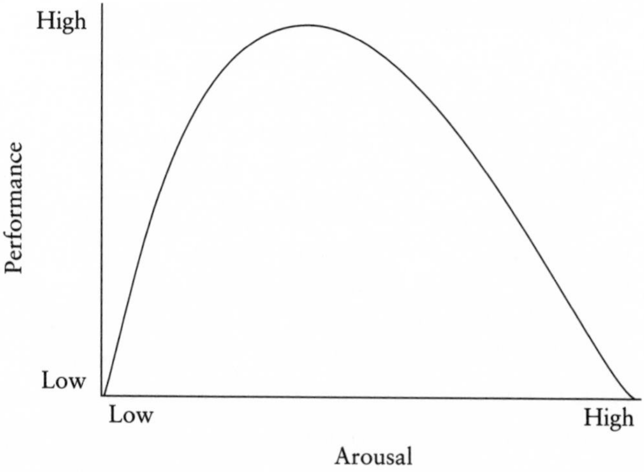

pinpoint exactly how much arousal leads to optimal performance. What does this all mean in tennis? It's clear that being either under- or overaroused will impair your performance. Optimal energy levels vary depending on the nature of the task and skill level of the performer. Studies have shown that more complex tasks require lower arousal levels, and that tennis requires more than "slight arousal" but less than "medium arousal." Other research demonstrates that highly skilled athletes and those performing simple tasks need a moderately high level of arousal for peak performance, whereas less skilled athletes and those performing complex tasks benefit more from a low level of arousal.

Since the demands in tennis are relatively complex, and tennis is a game of errors rather than winners, it's wise to heed scientific wisdom and guard against overarousal. This is especially true for beginners and intermediates! Using this same logic, professionals and those with more highly developed skills should benefit from slightly higher energy levels. The need to guard against high arousal in most tennis situations is reflected in Figure 5.2, where the curve leans clearly to the left.

The Catastrophe

Although the Inverted-U Theory has been widely accepted, some believe that it holds only when the athlete is not experiencing thoughts and feelings of anxiety. Under conditions of excessive worry, concern, or negativity, many assert that performance declines rather suddenly with increases in energy, and this drop in performance has been termed a "catastrophe." The catastrophe is illustrated in Figure 5.3. Smart tennis players guard very closely against any form of negative thinking so as to avoid the catastrophe. Once a catastrophe occurs, performance goes straight out the window!

The Reversal

Another popular view suggests that the key factor in determining how energy levels affect performance is the

Figure 5.3
The Catastrophe Theory in Tennis
(Under Conditions of Anxiety)

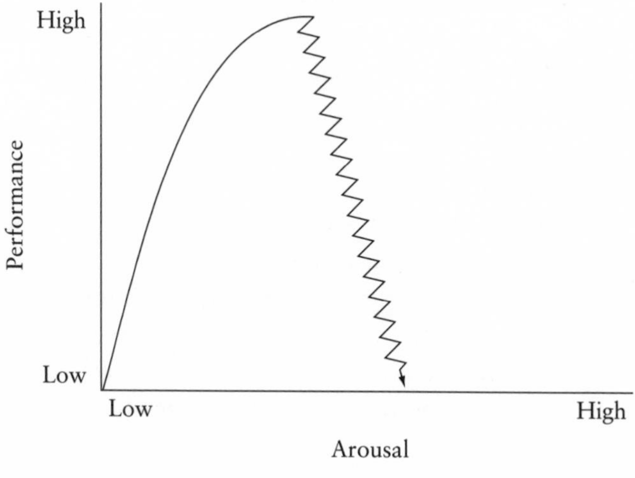

players' interpretation of their own arousal levels. The term "reversal" suggests that many athletes make quick changes (or reversals) in how they interpret energy levels. In one moment, energy previously interpreted as positive might suddenly be perceived as negative. This view highlights the importance of interpreting your sensations of energy in a positive manner. Increased energy is sometimes perceived as stressful, so it's important to reappraise these sensations as exciting energy inherent in competition, rather than as threats.

Energy-Related Problems and Solutions

Although mind-body fuel is widely available, just having energy is never enough. This power source must also be harnessed wisely. Energy can work wonders or throw you into chaos. Let's take a look at some of the more common energy problems, followed by smart tennis solutions.

Competitive Pressure

Competition breeds pressure. This is especially true in the unpredictable tennis environment where emergencies are often the rule rather than the exception. Some players feed off competitive pressure, improving their focus and raising their game to a higher level, while others allow themselves to be overwhelmed—at which point they choke and fold. How can individuals respond so very differently to the same demands?

Athletes at all levels experience heightened physiological arousal (butterflies, nervousness, perspiration) as a result of competitive pressure. These natural responses increase as the match becomes more meaningful and the ability levels of the players become more similar. These are normal results of sincere effort rather than pathological anxiety states. Evidence that competitive pressure can enhance performance is seen in the fact that most Olympic track records are broken in front of massive crowds, where pressure is greatest, rather than in practice.

Although performance is often improved following normal increases in energy and arousal, recall that the complexity of fine motor skills required in tennis dictates a guard against overarousal. As a result, responding to competitive pressure with additional increases in arousal due to worry, concern, or self-doubt inevitably destroys performance! It also steals attention away from what is important, wasting it on irrelevant fears.

It's unrealistic and perhaps fruitless to try to eliminate natural competitive pressure. However, studies suggest that the way an individual appraises stressful events determines whether the experienced emotion will be positive or negative. In other words, differences in the evaluation of competitive pressure situations, rather than the situations themselves, explain why some performers thrive while others wilt! Competitive pressure appraised as negative will inevitably lead to unhealthy anxiety and less proficient performance. In contrast, pressure welcomed as a necessary challenge and part of the thrill of competition guards against overarousal caused by needless worries, increases attention to the task at hand, and improves performance.

Courage is often caused by fear.
—French proverb

Here are some guidelines to help you manage the energy problems brought on by competitive pressure:

- Frequently play out points in practice. Training sessions should be as realistic as possible, with many competitive opportunities. By exposing yourself to competitive pressure, you'll teach yourself to manage it more effectively.
- Never allow your coach or practice partner to remain in one place too long and feed balls. This will only ensure that you become a great practice partner.
- Enter as many tournaments as you can to gain necessary experience in a competitive environment.
- Believe in yourself when the going gets rough. Nervous energy is a natural part of the game.

> Trust your preparation, stay focused, and hang in there to win the internal battle.

Welcome the uncertainty of competition as one of the most exciting parts of the performance. A good struggle is always fun! Competitive pressure is just a natural component of match play—embrace it eagerly to balance your energy and crush the demons of self-doubt and anxiety.

Lost Thrill

Although competition is usually sufficient motivation to keep you excited about performance, there are times when the thrill seems to vanish. Any frequently performed activity can lose its luster and appear routine, even a naturally challenging and exciting endeavor like tennis. Whether or not this seems likely to apply to you, I strongly advise you to monitor your heart for danger symptoms. No need to telephone your cardiologist, just periodically examine the desire, enthusiasm, and creativity you bring to the game. When these intangibles begin to fade, watch for energy and performance to slip too. Don't panic, just realize that minor adjustments, and perhaps some brief time away from the game, are required to restore the thrill.

Some external conditions contribute to boredom and staleness, including overtraining, rigid practice structures, or poor coaching, but your internal thoughts and feelings are most essential. Restoring the thrill of performance demands that you recognize that the real pleasure in any activity resides deep within your own psyche. True enthusiasm and joy come from within.

Reflect on your personal reasons for getting involved and remaining in this sport. Which self-expressions are facilitated by performing? What is most important and pleasurable to you as a person and as an athlete? If you are true to yourself, you will discover an inner drive and enthusiasm that knows few boundaries. It was really with you all along, but perhaps hidden for a while. Begin playing with renewed vitality and a purer mind-body fuel—and don't forget to check your heart on a regular basis.

Excessive Stress

Although tennis and other physical activities are excellent forms of stress relief, the serious competitive athlete often experiences stress similar to an ambitious corporate executive or a frazzled waitress. Too much stress can wreak havoc on your mind and body and destroy energy balance—resulting in frustration on the court, miserable play, or even twisted joints and strained muscles.

Players who shine in practice often crumble in tournaments because they manage stress poorly. Although optimal energy levels must be maintained for peak performance, prolonged arousal that cannot be reduced is never positive. Failing to prepare for stress is as unacceptable as forgetting to bring spare rackets to your match! Still, many players never invest in stress-busting tools.

Relaxation is one of the best means of reducing stress. There are as many relaxation programs on the market as there are diets. Most involve some combination of deep breathing, pleasant imagery, and muscular movements. Progressive Muscle Relaxation (PMR) is the "gold standard" of relaxation techniques, developed way back in 1929 and used to defeat a variety of physical and psychological ailments. PMR and its many variants are often used to prepare for competition and to manage stress during play.

PMR trains you to identify the relative contrast between muscular tension and the opposite sensation of complete calmness. By progressively tensing various muscles or muscle groups for several seconds and then completely releasing and relaxing them, you gradually learn to induce relaxation on demand during periods of high stress. Recognizing the contrast between tension and calmness is the key to success with PMR.

Two spin-offs of PMR are offered for smart tennis. The first involves a pre-match relaxation routine, and the second is a brief procedure for coping with stress in the heat of battle. Keep in mind that these methods will work for you only if you regularly practice and perfect them—you can't simply recall this page in a moment of stress and expect to get much use out of it.

Ten-Minute Pre-Match Stress Buster

Use the following minute-by-minute procedure to eliminate or reduce stress prior to the actual match.

Minute 1

The big performance is upon you. Before the warm-up, find a quiet place and comfortable position where you will not be disturbed. Close your eyes and relax totally, but do not fall asleep.

Minute 2

Inhale for six to eight seconds deeply and slowly, then exhale for ten to twelve seconds. Continue this breathing pattern throughout the whole routine.

Minutes 3 through 8

While breathing in, tense a muscle group and hold it tight for the duration of the inhalation. Totally and immediately release all muscular tension upon exhalation. Study, interpret, and examine the contrast between the sensations of tension and relaxation. Spend about two minutes for muscle groups in each major region of the body (upper, middle, and lower). Vary the exact muscles used as you see fit, but always focus on the difference between unpleasantly tight tension and its total opposite, peaceful relaxation.

Minutes 9 and 10

Now that your awareness of relaxing sensations is heightened, visualize yourself performing to perfection. (See Chapter Three for guidelines on imagery.) After you finish, stretch out and fire yourself up for a great performance.

On-Court Stress Buster

Now you are deep in the heat of a match and feel that stress is intruding. Accept that you are stressed, but reinterpret these sensations as the normal and exciting consequences of caring about the match. In between points, breathe deeply and slowly while tensing those muscles that have been most affected by the stress (often the shoulder muscles). As before, release all tension immediately upon slow exhalation. Visualize your prematch routine (Stress Buster One) and all the pleasant sensations elicited by the procedure, then image your next point to perfection.

Excessive stress will destroy proper energy balance, but you now have two very simple means of coping with stress and restoring the balance in tennis and other situations too. Remember that for these routines to work properly, they must be practiced and perfected. Adjust these stress busters to suit your particular needs. If you're still having problems with excessive stress, seek the services of a qualified professional.

Proper Breathing

Although breathing seems like such a natural function, improper breathing is quite common in sports and causes severe problems with energy management. It's easy to lose control of your respiration during times of heightened arousal in competition. Irregular breathing leads to overactivation that sabotages the fine muscular coordination needed in tennis and other skilled acts. It can also result in a reduction of oxygen, which can lead to emotional as well as physical distress.

There's a real survival benefit in becoming quickly energized. Humans evolved to cope with imminent threats to life such as aggressive tigers. Thus, life-threatening situations produced rapid increases in respiration, activating large muscle groups to escape fast or fight the aggressor. Unfortunately, this sudden energy burst does little for your delicately placed volley in the twenty-first century. Perhaps in the next major stage of human evolution, with fewer tigers and more tennis prize money for survival, we'll develop the ability to direct more energy into the fine motor skills needed for tennis!

In any performance situation it's important to monitor breathing quality. In competitive tennis, breathing patterns often fluctuate wildly from point to point, destroying rhythm and coordination and reducing energy. Although lower brain regions control respiration, a few glitches in the system remain when it comes to tennis.

Breath control in tennis needs to be learned, practiced, and refined.

Here are some specific tips to help control your breathing in tennis:

- Synchronize breathing precisely with hitting the ball. Breathe in from the nose as the ball is coming and exhale from the mouth upon contact. Practice this regularly and it will become natural in the match.
- Maintain a continuous breathing pattern regardless of the situation. There is a tendency to tighten up and hold your breath under pressure. Resist this urge through practice and regular attention to your respiration quality.
- When possible, inhalations should be slow, smooth, rhythmic, and from deep in the lower region of your stomach. This allows greater amounts of oxygen to be taken in and prevents the kind of short, rapid breathing that can occur in panic situations.
- Use exhalations as a signal to hit crisp and accurate shots. Destroy the ball with your breath!
- Before a difficult match, or when you're nervous, take extra care to keep your breathing continuous, deliberate, slow, and smooth. By

focusing on your breathing you'll also distract yourself from worries.

- Changeovers are a good time to moderate your breathing pattern by taking slow and deep breaths followed by even slower exhalations.
- Another good time to focus on breathing is before serving and receiving. Gain control over your oxygen intake before the point and maintain it throughout the point.

Now that you've learned a few tips to improve your breath control, you have the tools to become a more controlled player with greater energy efficiency. Nervousness is not negative in itself, but uncontrolled respiration is.

Anger

Although anger can be transformed into productive energy, it more often sabotages performance. Let's take a look at the problem of anger and offer some smart tennis solutions.

Anger is an emotional reaction combining high energy and high stress. Other definitions include "strong displeasure and hostility aroused by a real or suspected wrong," "a response to the frustration of an unresolved problem," and "a sudden violent displeasure accompanied by an impulse to retaliate." Although expressed anger is easy to recognize, angry thoughts and feelings may exist internally, well concealed from others.

Anger intensity varies widely. Whereas irritation and annoyance are forms of mild anger, strongly emotional and energetic anger is sometimes called rage. Fury is rage so great that it resembles insanity. It's important to distinguish between the normal anger that occurs during competition and the much more serious anger that may extend beyond sport and lead to serious physical and emotional harm. People who observe themselves beginning to approach the serious levels of anger are strongly advised to seek counseling.

Tennis was traditionally associated with the gracious manners and refined etiquette of the elite. As a result, expressions of anger were vigorously repressed in favor of style and sportsmanship. This gentler and kinder time has all but vanished, and tennis is now embraced by irate masses worldwide, cultivated or not! Expressions of anger are witnessed at all levels of many sports in screaming, temper tantrums, cursing, equipment throwing, abuse of officials, and self-condemnation. Anger contained within can be equally disruptive when the player is consumed by negative thoughts and images.

Uncontrolled anger is a form of energy that almost always impairs performance. One explanation is that arousal levels rise dangerously high, throwing off fine motor control and attention. Keep in mind that tennis requires relatively low energy levels compared with most other sports.

Controlled anger sometimes proves useful on the tennis courts. It's uncertain whether John McEnroe will be best remembered for his raw talent or his wildly theatrical tantrums. He was actually a brilliant strategist who used anger to distract opponents while maintaining internal control. Perhaps he wasn't angry at all, and it often seemed to give him an advantage. I'm not recommending that anger be used this way—just warning you to stay extra focused when your opponent gets mad!

Getting mad at yourself after unforced errors might sometimes be useful, because it shows that you value consistency. But stay in control and move mentally to the next point or you'll find yourself distracted and unable to perform at your best.

Here are some further ways to control anger:

- Use your anger to focus intensely on what you'll do next rather than on the mistake you just made.
- Learn to recognize negative self-talk immediately when it happens—it's a killer on the court. Use this increased awareness as a means of further motivating yourself to transform negative thoughts into more positive ones.
- Do whatever it takes to break the pattern when anger is overwhelming you. Tie your shoelaces,

count to ten, breathe deeply and slowly, or walk slowly to the fence. Whatever you do, get yourself in the mind-set of playing each point one at a time.

- Use imagery to practice dealing with situations that have caused anger in the past. Imagine yourself handling these situations gracefully.

Energy Regulation

Applying the right mixture of energy to your performances is an ongoing challenge, especially if the TMBC in Chapter One indicated that you should focus on this chapter for improvement! Since individual differences prevail, there are no fast and ready rules that will work for everyone. It's necessary to assess your own energy patterns and resulting performance. One way to accomplish this is to practice increasing and decreasing arousal in various dimensions, noting the effects on performance. Players like Bjorn Borg and Arthur Ashe seemed to perform exceptionally well by remaining calm whereas others like Andre Agassi and Martina Hingis appear to require much higher energy levels. Energy patterns vary just as much as playing styles and racket designs.

The following are some techniques used to modify energy levels in the four dimensions of physical sensations, emotions, thoughts, and actions. You should develop many others too.

To energize physical sensations: Increase your rhythm and rate of breathing; stretch and exercise more before playing; jump during play.

To decrease energy from physical sensations: Breathe deeply and slowly from low in the stomach; engage in muscle relaxation, briefly tensing and relaxing muscle groups, and noting the contrast between tension and relaxation.

To energize emotions: Listen to upbeat music prior to play; draw energy from the crowd.

To decrease energy from emotions: Listen to relaxing and soothing music; visualize a calm and relaxing scene.

To energize thoughts: Smile and remind yourself that you love to compete; rehearse your match strategy, anticipating many competitive scenarios and your best responses to them.

To decrease energy from thoughts: Think in slow motion while breathing slowly and deeply; engage in your favorite form of meditation; quietly repeat a calming word to yourself (something like "easy" or "cool"); direct your focus to performance rather than outcome.

To energize actions: Pump your fist or use a similar energizing gesture during play (remain polite!); visualize powerful forces (such as a leaping cheetah or a rocket blast); distract yourself from fatigue and focus on the task at hand.

To decrease energy from actions: Dictate a slower match pace by taking your time between points; use a methodical ritual (for example, bounce the ball before serving) to add consistency and prevent rapid movements; breathe deeply and slowly from low in your stomach.

Specific Tips for Improving Energy Control

Here is a brief overview of this chapter to help you gain better energy control. This section can be used when you are short on time and just want to review the important points in finding the right balance of power!

- Regulate your energy levels, controlling your overall arousal and also the way you allocate that arousal among thoughts, emotions, physical sensations, and actions.
- Guard against using excessive energy in tennis—most tennis skills require only low to moderate amounts of arousal.
- Tap into active mood states, determination, competitive excitement, physical well-being, social influences, confidence and self-esteem, and imagery and self-talk as sources of energy to use as mind-body fuel.

- Guard against all forms of negative thinking to avoid catastrophic reductions in performance with increasing energy levels.
- Interpret increasing energy levels as a positive benefit of sport and enjoy the excitement of competitive pressure.
- Remember that performance declines with the onset of boredom or staleness. When this happens, take a brief break, if needed, and then look deeply within yourself to find the joy that has temporarily vanished. Take measures to regain the interest and challenge, and performance will return too.
- Use both the Ten-Minute Pre-Match Stress Buster and the On-Court Stress Buster found in this chapter to cope with stress through relaxation.
- Regulate your breathing patterns through the steps outlined in the Proper Breathing section in this chapter.
- Learn to control your anger and use it to motivate you toward higher achievement—otherwise it's apt to impair your performance.
- Find your own optimal arousal level by adjusting energy levels in each of the four dimensions. You'll know when you're optimally energized!

Energy can do great wonders or inflict great harm. Your mind-body fuel is no exception. The search for the right balance of power is an ongoing and worthy quest that never ceases, leading only to higher performance. Make it a goal to find your own optimal energy levels—your play will surely improve, whatever its current level.

Speaking of worthwhile goals, Chapter Six helps you set and achieve them. Goal setting is a motivational strategy that puts you on the right course for success.

6

Goal Setting

Masterminding Achievement

Before the tennis season, fourteen-year-old Lillian McIsaacs and her coach-father, Bernard, set realistic performance goals. Their ultimate goal for the season was to qualify for the Texas state regional junior tennis championships. The family lived in one of the poorer parts of Houston, a community that only had one concrete tennis court at the public park, and many of the girls Lillian played against in the Houston city league regarded the championships as an unreachable goal for her. Despite the sarcasm and cynicism of others in the league, however, Lillian practiced hard. She studied her opponents, concentrated on specific performance goals in every match, and played in a number of tournaments outside Houston. A little past halfway through the season, Lillian rose to a number

10 ranking in the state. She continued to do well for the balance of the year and ended up ranked third overall. Because of her ranking, she was invited to the Texas southern regional championships.

In her first match she couldn't get on track. Uncharacteristically, she found herself making tentative shots and double faults, and her net game was nonexistent. She'd lost the match 6–1, 6–2 and had been eliminated. A feeling of disappointment enveloped her. "I don't know, I just didn't have it today," she said. "I thought I was ready, but I guess I wasn't."

Her dad nodded in agreement. "You weren't prepared for championship performance today," he said. "You didn't have your usual drive to win. And I think I know why."

Lillian looked up at him, surprised. "You do?"

"We failed to prepare for the championships, and that prepared us for failure," he said. "Our goal this year was to play well enough to be invited to the regionals. Once we reached that goal, our motivation was satisfied. We neglected to adjust our season's ultimate goal when it looked certain that you would earn a place at the regionals. Without a more difficult yet reachable goal, it's no wonder that you were unable to get motivated to your usual competitive level."

She looked down, embarrassed and saddened that she had not been able to motivate herself to a higher level of performance. Her father put his arm around her.

"We'll both know better next year," he said with a smile. She slowly looked up, and a smile spread across her face as well.

That night, as she fell asleep, Lillian imagined herself receiving the trophy for the State championship. She made a note to visit with her dad in the morning to lay out the goals that would have to be attained for her new dream to become reality.

Although Lillian was a hard worker and an exceptionally talented athlete, she still had much to learn about goals. Goal setting is a powerful motivational strategy—and a smart plan. Knowing how goals benefit you and the proper ways to set and achieve them is essential. It's really the art of developing and following a plan that will take you where you want to go. Simply knowing what you want (say, winning your club's championship) is never enough, and players often set goals improperly or just fail to set them at all. Smart tennis players set and achieve goals based on scientific principles and experience. This chapter places you on the highway to achievement.

Goal setting can be used to improve any area of performance including mind-body skills such as imagery and attention control. The benefits of proper goal setting were evident in a player I recently worked with. She was experiencing anxiety in close matches, dwelling on the outcome, and playing too conservatively in the third set. Several months after working out a goal setting program with her, she commented on her progress:

I'm thinking more realistically about only what I can control, worrying less about losing, and striving harder when the going gets rough. I also stay more relaxed and focused.

The advantages of proper goal setting for this player were evident in her actions (striving harder), thoughts (more realistic), emotions (less worried), and physical sensations (more relaxed). She discovered a purpose that was missing before she embraced goal setting, and her play improved. Goal setting is no secret, but few players use this strategy to their full advantage. Let's take a closer look.

Definition of Goals

Goals are defined as something we deliberately want to achieve or accomplish, and these targets give our energies specific direction. Goal setting provides a sense of control over actions and allows us to move beyond beliefs or fears that may be preventing us from realizing our peak performance. Since there are always countless activities to choose from, goals clarify what is important and provide real purpose.

Achievement Awareness

Since goals are a way of maximizing achievement, let's engage in a brief self-analysis to determine what achievement means to you. Do you view achievement primarily as defeating others and demonstrating superior competence? Or as improving your skills and getting to the next level regardless of competitive outcome? Think about this a moment. If you chose the second approach, you're on your way toward maximizing the effectiveness of goal setting. This approach is called *task involvement.* Task-involved athletes have been shown to display high intrinsic motivation. That is, they are motivated by personal and internal reasons such as fun or pride rather than by external rewards such as money or recognition. They also produce greater effort and persist longer than other athletes in a variety of performance situations. They set goals to master skills. On the other hand, the first approach is called *ego-involvement.* Ego-involved athletes define their performance in comparison with others. This approach appears to work best only when you're completely confident of your abilities and not threatened by the possibility of losing. Unfortunately, many ego-involved athletes also avoid challenging situations that might otherwise take them to a higher level.

Arriving at one goal is the starting point to another.
—John Dewey

Your philosophy of achievement often directs the type of goals you'll set. Research indicates that performance goals (such as a higher first serve percentage) are usually superior to outcome goals (such as winning the tournament). In my opinion, focusing too much on "winning" is an irrelevant distraction. As I discussed in Chapter Two, you need to save your attention for more specific things. Rather than worrying about winning or losing, stay interested in improving your performance. The outcome will take care of itself. We'll talk about motivation shortly.

Advantages of Setting Goals

There are many advantages to setting goals. Let's examine some of the real benefits in tennis—and many other situations too. If you're not convinced of goal setting's benefits after reviewing these ten advantages, you probably never will be!

- *Improved play.* There's no question that proper goal setting improves performance. The key word, however, is *proper.* This chapter will ensure that you are setting top-quality goals for top performance.
- *Improved practice.* Practice is often wasted on activities that don't translate into improvement. By setting and achieving goals in practice, you'll

be more disciplined and focused on activities that make you better.

- *Understanding of expectations.* Having a target lets you know exactly where to place your energies. This takes uncertainty out of your performances, reminding you where you are and where you're going.
- *Challenge and excitement.* As mentioned in Chapter Five, there are times when the thrill of the game seems to vanish. Setting goals that are difficult yet attainable adds challenge and excitement to keep you moving ahead.
- *Higher intrinsic motivation.* Self-generated and internalized goals are better motivators than having to follow another person's agenda. By creating and believing in your own goals you'll be driven from deep within, and this is a rich source of energy.
- *Fulfillment and confidence.* Setting and achieving goals provides fulfillment. As your performances improve, self-confidence rises too. For a review of this relationship, take a look at Chapter Four.
- *Reduced anxiety.* As noted in Chapter Five, anxiety is a poor source of energy. When you set and achieve smart goals, you have no room for needless fears and concerns. You'll be too absorbed in your quest. Of course, goals need to

be reasonably attainable or you could become anxious. We'll talk about this in just a minute.

- *Improved concentration.* Having clear aims and objectives helps maintain attention over time. Without a clear plan, it's easy to allow harmful distractions to intrude, and to lose focus.
- *Sense of purpose.* Hitting a fluffy yellow ball over a three-foot net can be fun, but let's hope there's more to it than that! Goals make it all the more meaningful and set you on a mission to achieve.
- *Better search for strategies.* With exact objectives in mind (say, less than twenty unforced errors in a match), you'll work harder and smarter for solutions. There are many roads to achievement, and committing to goals encourages you to find the best strategies to take you there.

You may be able to come up with additional advantages to setting and systematically working toward your goals. Figure 6.1 summarizes these ten advantages.

Paving the Way to Effective Goal Setting

Having discussed some key benefits associated with goal setting, let's set a foundation from which successful goal setting can be conducted. There are several important principles to keep in mind while embarking on a journey toward achievement. These include a per-

Figure 6.1
Ten Benefits of Setting Goals

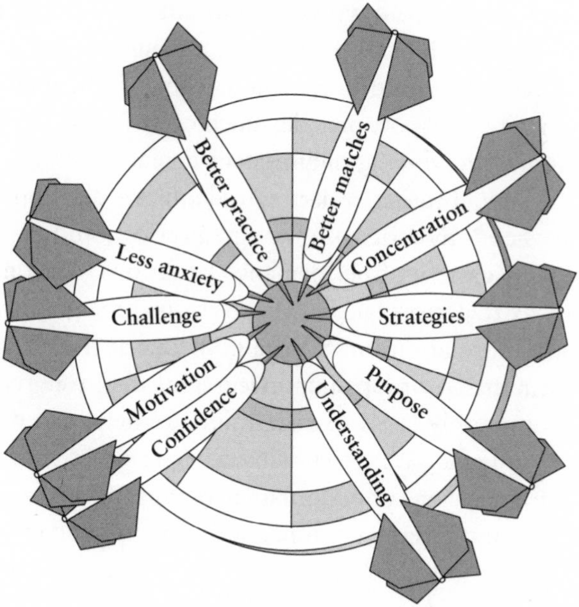

formance focus, proper motivation, nonperfectionistic thinking, and competitiveness.

Place Performance Above Winning

Wouldn't it be great if there were a special place where every player won every match? In this tennis fantasyland, scores would be meaningless since every player would be crowned champion. If this is what you seek, keep on dreaming. When you wake up and smell the coffee again, you'll remember that every player loses except the one who wins the tournament. Without the risk of losing, however, your dream would probably be so boring it would keep you asleep! Challenge and uncertainty in sport provide much of the thrill. An obsession with winning only hastens defeat.

As noted earlier, task-involved athletes display high intrinsic motivation, produce great effort, and persist across a variety of performance situations. They also emphasize performance goals over outcome goals and retain more attention for the immediate challenge at hand. Getting wrapped up in thoughts about scores or outcomes only leads to distraction, anxiety, and pressure. You really want to be sincerely fascinated with the many dimensions of performance. Staying excited about performance keeps you firmly in the present and guards against the loss of self-confidence that could occur when the next Pete Sampras or Venus Williams strolls into town. On the other hand, these players might make even the best players question their self-confidence!

Take a few seconds to recall the best performance of your life. You may not remember the details well because you were so perfectly absorbed in the moment. Expending energy dwelling on past mistakes or possible outcomes would only have spoiled this peak experience. Your focus on performance that day was admirable and winning took care of itself. This is where you want to be every match. Ways of setting performance goals will be discussed later in the chapter. Figure 6.2 illustrates the difference between having a "winning focus" and a "performance focus."

Success Motivation

It has long been recognized that inner desire and drive are required for successful performance. What is the essence of the quest for dominance? Why do athletes tenaciously struggle to refine technique, improve strategy,

Figure 6.2
"Winning Focus" Versus "Performance Focus"

and strive for the summit? Let's take a look at several factors underlying the motivation to achieve, and how these elements may affect your performance.

Achievement behavior is traditionally seen as influenced by a blend of *hope for success* and *fear of failure.* In sports, some athletes are primarily motivated to succeed, while others are more inspired to avoid failure. Take a moment to consider which of these two possibilities motivates you the most. Does hope for success or fear of failure lead to higher levels of motivation for you?

One traditional view holds that when the tendency to avoid failure is greater than the tendency to succeed, maximum motivation occurs when the outcome of the competitive event is almost 100 percent certain (either winning against a much weaker opponent or losing against a much stronger opponent). In these situations, athletes have little chance of losing face—even a loss to a superior opponent is expected and would not be evaluated as failure. When the outcome of the event is less certain (that is, ability levels are more similar), motivation should decline because there is a real chance of perceived failure. On the other hand, when the tendency to succeed surpasses the tendency to avoid failure, the greatest motivation occurs in highly competitive situations where the outcome is uncertain due to more similar ability levels. Athletes who approach success derive great satisfaction from the pursuit without worrying about the possibility of failure. They are success oriented! They may become bored against much weaker opponents and apathetic when they have little chance of winning—but when the battle heats up, these are the real competitors.

In my opinion, it's very important to develop a motivation to succeed because it gives you a focus that is positive, goal oriented, and anxiety reducing. Excessive fear of failure is a great impediment to success. With that weight removed, athletes are free to aggressively seek success. A slight dose of "fear of failure," however, is a helpful guard against overconfidence when you expect to win easily.

Here are a few tips to help you develop and nurture the motivation to succeed:

- Search for the success elements in every competitive encounter. Short-term performance goals provide an excellent way of identifying factors needed for continual improvement. Attaining these goals provides a rewarding sense of satisfaction, regardless of competitive outcome.
- Get excited and enjoy the competition when it's close. Thrive on being challenged, for it brings out your best and allows you the chance to achieve greater victories.
- Never be afraid to "go for it!" Whether this involves hitting a decisive topspin passing shot

under pressure or throwing a well-timed touchdown pass with three seconds left, the habit of assuming control and making things happen is the mark of a champion.

Eliminate Perfectionism

If you're an athlete, coach, or parent, you might believe that success could only be achieved through the most complete and total pursuit of excellence. You might also think that perfectionism is the key to unlocking the door to untold riches, and that those who fall short of perfection are doomed to mediocrity and shame. If these two statements characterize your views on performance, or if you know someone adhering to these assumptions, then read on. It's perhaps ironic that perfectionism leads neither to higher performance nor to happiness. In fact, perfectionism can destroy your success and enjoyment of sport and lead to general problems too. Let's examine the curse of perfectionism and offer tips on breaking this pattern so as to clear the way for proper goal setting and true success.

> Seeking excellence is inspiring; seeking perfection is demoralizing.
>
> —Anonymous ex-perfectionist

In any performance situation, it's healthy to want to do your best. You hone your technical skills by paying attention to coaching, improve your mind-body skills through sport psychology, and condition your body with specific training and nutritional strategies. This pursuit of high standards and emphasis on quality is a prerequisite of true accomplishment and should be encouraged. However, when you slip over the line into perfectionism and set standards beyond reach or reason, measuring life entirely in terms of productivity and accomplishment, the drive to excel becomes self-defeating, dangerous, and maladaptive.

Perfectionists believe that if they fail to perform flawlessly, they will be embarrassed, disgraced, and doomed. They irrationally believe that they must be perfect to be accepted by others. They see winning 6–1, 6–1 as blowing two games because they were less than perfect, and losing closely as grounds for humiliation and self-exile. No success is enough to appreciate for itself; winning simply leads to higher and more unrealistic goals. Life becomes an endless pursuit of acceptance through performance. Fear of failure looms larger and larger, as focus is often directed on past failures rather than accomplishments. Rather than setting goals and viewing competition with positive energy and an eager attitude of challenge, perfectionists make self-statements such as, "I cannot fail, because if I fail I am totally worthless."

Some wonder whether perfectionism enhances performance, especially in competitive societies where "winning at all costs" thinking predominates. If perfectionism really worked, I'd devote a full section to its pursuit. But that's far from the case—studies indicate that perfectionists actually succeed less than their less rigid counterparts and are less skilled in their sports!

Successful perfectionists appear to achieve their success despite perfectionism rather than because of it.

OK, so you've identified someone (maybe yourself) as a perfectionist. So what! You want to win, you'll do anything to succeed, and you'll consider yourself useless if you don't. Is there a more serious price to pay by adopting this stance? Here are some of the problems associated with perfectionism:

- Many forms of physical illness—coronary artery disease, for one—are more prevalent among individuals with perfectionist tendencies.
- Mood disorders such as anxiety and depression are common among perfectionists. Intense self-criticism leads to intolerance of others who fail to meet unrealistically high standards, often resulting in resentment and relationship difficulties.
- Focusing on flaws and mistakes depletes energy. This may escalate to panic-like states prior to competition, impairing smooth performance.
- Creativity is destroyed and learning stunted by not trying newer and perhaps riskier methods.

Excessive self-criticism takes the enjoyment out of sport and life.

To change long-established behavioral patterns and personality characteristics, it might be necessary to enlist the support and services of a qualified professional. Such habits, beliefs, and traits never change overnight; but acceptance of a problem is a first step.

If you perceive yourself as a perfectionist, I hope you'll agree that being a perfectionist is a no-win proposition. How do you go about changing? Here are a few tips to help you do so.

- Change your absolute standards and begin appreciating even minor successes by setting lower goals.
- Realize that others are less interested in how you might perform than you think. Accept yourself as worthy of the same amount of acceptance regardless of how well you perform.
- Focus on the enjoyable aspects of the sport. Try to appreciate performance and let the outcome take care of itself.
- Allow yourself to make mistakes. Think of long-term improvement rather than immediate success or failure.
- Ignore the outcome completely and simply try to achieve one performance goal (for example,

hit four more winners from the baseline each match).

Perfectionism is not all it's cracked up to be, and it's far from a prerequisite for optimal performance. On the contrary, this compulsion is harmful to your athletic performance and enjoyment in life. Stop being so perfect and you'll find the keys to real success!

Increase Your Competitiveness

Although perfectionism is not useful, healthy competitiveness is normal in sport and will help you achieve your goals. What does it mean to say that an athlete displayed outstanding competitiveness? How can you become more competitive and successful in tennis?

For many tennis players and fans, "competitiveness" evokes memories of Jimmy Connors's never-say-die perseverance or John McEnroe's cleverly timed outbursts. Sport psychologists use this term to describe much more than extreme desire or tactics. From this perspective, competitiveness involves the whole range of attitudes, thoughts, feelings, and behavior associated with the pursuit of excellence and the long-term journey of getting there. Combined with proper goal setting, competitiveness makes athletes hard to stop!

Competitiveness has also been described as achievement motivation. Recall our previous discussion on the advantages of striving for success over attempting to avoid failure. Although we all desire optimal performance, match outcome is actually impossible to control.

How do you explain your wins and losses to yourself? Sport psychology studies have proven that these self-explanations are closely related to your level of competitiveness and future performance. Highly competitive performers believe that success results from stable factors such as talent and ability, and internal factors such as effort and health. On the contrary, less effective competitors attribute success to unstable factors such as luck and external factors such as opponent weakness. The message here is to give yourself full credit for your wins without minimizing your part in a successful performance. This will increase your confidence and motivation for your next match.

Highly competitive performers attribute failure to unstable factors such as poor strategy and external factors such as opponent strength. Players low in competitiveness ascribe failure to stable factors such as low ability and internal factors such as reduced interest. After a failure, it's in your interest to credit the opponent's performance but realize that conditions can easily change the next time to increase your chances for success. This will keep you hungry and positive in your pursuit of goals for the next match.

Maintaining proper competitiveness involves a number of factors. Make sure that you're placing most of your emphasis on task goals rather than outcome goals.

Remember that focusing on winning does little to help you win. Anticipate the enjoyment and thrill of competition and learn to love the chance to play in front of others. Find opponents that are near your own ability level, or slightly better, and thrive on situations where there is a legitimate chance of losing. Never walk away from a healthy challenge.

Finally, learn to control your explanations for winning and losing and you'll be more competitive in your next match. When you're really looking forward to the excitement of the match, your competitiveness may even scare your opponent!

Goal Setting in Action

Let's move forward and put goal setting into action. The next sections present guidelines to help you implement goal setting in a smart tennis manner. Use copies of the goal setting worksheet at the end of this chapter to assist in planning, adjusting, and achieving your goals.

Identify Your Dreams

The first step is to determine what you'd ideally like to accomplish. Get a piece of paper and pencil and allow yourself to wander into a fantasy world where nothing is impossible. What are your dreams for performance over the next twelve months? Write down your top five dreams. Dreams are a great source of motivation and provide a long-term focus that is extremely important. Now, examine the five dreams you listed and ask yourself if they're all realistic. Can you really hope to accomplish these within twelve months? Be honest with yourself and eliminate the impossible ones. For example, if you are number five on your Division II college team, it's unrealistic to set a goal to win Wimbledon next year! On the other hand, it might be reasonable to aim for the number two position on your squad. Similarly, a 3.5 level player hoping to reach the 5.0 level within one year needs a reality check! Keep on brainstorming until you've arrived at three realistic dreams for the upcoming year.

Identify Performance Goals

Congratulations on discovering three realistic dreams. These are now your long-range goals. The next step is to identify the performance goals that will help you achieve these end results. Remember that too much focus on the outcome is a distraction that offers little in the way of improvement. The best way to realize positive outcomes is by having a narrower and more task-appropriate focus.

For each of your three long-range goals, write down five performance goals that will help take you there in the next twelve months. These are the activities from which you'll develop short-range goals. If your goal is to move up three places on your college team, two performance goals might be to improve your first service percentage from 50 percent to 70 percent and decrease your unforced errors by ten each match. The performance goals you identify should be realistic yet challenging, specific, and measurable. As a performance goal, "do your best" is not very helpful because it provides nothing specific and cannot be easily measured. On the other hand, a goal to reduce the number of negative self-statements you make each set from ten to two is a very clear goal that can be measured and recorded.

How challenging should your performance goals be? Although there are no precise answers, one rule of thumb is to set performance goals that you can achieve about 55 percent of the time. If you are reaching your goals more than 70 percent of the time, set higher goals. If you're achieving your goals less than 40 percent of the time, make them easier. In addition to physical performance goals, it's also appropriate to set performance goals involving any of the mind-body strategies discussed in this book.

Make a Schedule

Now that you've identified three long-range dream goals and fifteen underlying performance goals, it's time to create a schedule that will lead you toward your dreams.

Break each of your fifteen performance subgoals into an intermediate quarterly goal (every three months). For example, if you plan on increasing your approaches to the net by sixteen over the next year, you might develop a schedule to approach the net four more times per match within the next three months. Write down your quarterly performance goal deadlines on the worksheet at the end of this chapter.

Now further break your performance goals down into monthly, weekly, and daily short-range goals, and record these on worksheets too. After you've completed the worksheets, you'll have devised a plan to achieve your long-range objectives within the next year!

With daily, weekly, monthly, and quarterly goals established, you're well on your way toward improvement. Half the battle is just knowing what you need to accomplish each day. Pay close attention to your daily activities and make sure they're in line with the goals you've set. Use the imagery techniques in Chapter Three to visualize yourself completing the goals you've established for each day.

After setting your goals, give yourself at least two weeks before making any major adjustments. After the two-week period, reevaluate your goals to make sure they're still reasonable. If not, adjust them as needed. Continue reevaluating your goals every two weeks, making further adjustments as necessary.

Remain Flexible

It's important to remain flexible in your approach to goal setting! Initially you might find it somewhat difficult—your goals will probably be either too hard or too easy. This is normal. Simply adjust your goals as necessary. The more goals you set, the more accurate you'll become in setting goals that are attainable but also challenging enough to motivate you. Goals should ideally lead to steady progression and improvement, but recall from Chapter Four that progress often occurs with minor steps backward along the way (see Figure 4.3). You may stumble many times along the way, but your goal setting techniques will get better over time! The key is to keep moving forward with your plans.

Specific Tips for Setting and Achieving Goals

Although there are no exact rules to follow in goal setting, let's review the guiding principles that have been effective in maximizing performance by using this achievement-producing technique. This section can be used as a brief review to ensure that you are making progress intelligently.

- Set goals for all kinds of technical skills as well as mind-body skills such as imagery, attention control, and confidence.

- Set specific, measurable goals with a target date for completion. Goals that are vague (such as "do your best") or without deadlines are not very useful.
- Set long-range, intermediate, and short-range goals. Although long-range dream goals are a source of great motivation, short-term and intermediate goals keep you in check and help monitor progress.
- Set difficult yet attainable goals that push you toward your limits. Easy goals tend to reduce effort, and goals that are too hard can lead to discouragement.
- Place most of your emphasis on performance goals rather than outcome goals. Thinking too much about winning is a distraction.
- Set goals for practice as well as for match play.
- Reevaluate your goals periodically and adjust them as necessary.
- Strive to achieve success rather than to avoid failure, but use fear of failure occasionally as a guard against overconfidence.
- Steer clear of perfectionistic thinking.
- View achievement primarily as a way of improving your own skills rather than demonstrating superiority over others. Winning takes care of itself.

Goal setting is a mind-body tool that acts as a powerful source of motivation. Your actions are more deliberate and effective when you know where you've been and where you're going, and have a plan to take you there.

Chapter Seven shows you how to bring all the mind-body skills together to play smart tennis. You'll be directed to winning activities before, during, and after your match.

Your Goal-Setting Worksheet

Your goal setting program should suit your needs as a smart tennis player. Copy these sheets as you see fit, and have fun setting and achieving goals that lead to success. Remember, this is just a starting point. Create your own system and change the time parameters as you see fit. For example, you might want to establish a goal setting program that includes two goals over a period of four months rather than three in a year—do whatever will work for your own game!

A. List your top five dreams for performance over the next twelve months. Anything goes!

   1. ______________________________

   2. ______________________________

   3. ______________________________

   4. ______________________________

   5. ______________________________

B. Now evaluate the dreams you've listed. Are they realistic? More carefully select three dreams that can be achieved over the next twelve months. These are your long-range goals:

   1. ______________________________

   2. ______________________________

   3. ______________________________

C. Now list five performance goals to be achieved over the next twelve months to help you accomplish each long-range goal. Make sure that each behavior is specific, measurable, and difficult (yet attainable).

Goal: ______________________________

1. ______________________________

2. ______________________________

3. ______________________________

4. ______________________________

5. ______________________________

Goal: ______________________________

1. ______________________________

2. ______________________________

3. ______________________________

4. ______________________________

5. ______________________________

Goal: ______________________________

1. ______________________________

2. ______________________________

3. ______________________________

4. ______________________________

5. ______________________________

D. Break each performance goal down into what needs to be done in the next three months and record these steps on separate goal setting sheets. These are your quarterly performance goals.

E. Establish monthly performance goals and record them on separate goal setting sheets.

F. Establish weekly performance goals and record them on separate goal setting sheets.

G. Establish daily performance goals and record them on separate goal setting sheets.

H. You should now have separate sheets for quarterly, monthly, weekly, and daily performance goals. Label them accordingly and place them in a folder for easy reference.

I. Keep in mind the importance of flexibility and adjustment. Every two weeks evaluate your goals and make changes if needed to keep you moving forward. There is no shame in decreasing or increasing the difficulty level of your goals. Feel free to select improved goals as you see fit. Have fun as you accomplish your objectives!

7

Competition Management

Playing Smart Tennis

A strong wind swirled around the court as Ben Matthews prepared to serve in the first game of the Fisher, Illinois, Senior Tennis Festival. The festival, a major fundraiser for the small community's medical center, was something Ben had been looking forward to for about six months. In the preceding year's competition he'd done quite well for a player who had only started tennis three years earlier. From a field of sixteen entrants in the sixty-five-and-over age bracket, Ben had placed sixth. Although some small part of him hoped to do as well or better this year, it wasn't a higher tournament placing that fueled his desire to start today's competition.

The festival allowed him to meet old friends, play against other senior players from Fisher (as well as a handful of really good players from the Champaign-Urbana area), and contribute to a worthy charity. Ben knew that these were all good reasons to look forward to this year's competition, but there was more to it this year. Although Ben viewed the festival as a friendly competition, he knew that it was also a place where he could test, in a real competition, the new mental skills he'd been working on over the last half year. He knew that he would find out at the festival if everything he'd studied about the psychology of tennis would make a difference not only in his placing in the competition, but in his ability to perform up to the new performance standards he'd set for himself.

About six months earlier, Ben had stumbled across an article in an Internet tennis magazine that talked about how important the mental game was to all athletes. That had led him to the few books he could find on the mental aspects of the game, and to seeking the advice of a sport psychologist at the University of Illinois. Convinced that he'd been overlooking an important aspect of his tennis training, Ben wholeheartedly began to examine every aspect of mental training as it applied to tennis.

The first thing he'd done, at the advice of the sport psychologist, was to understand his personal needs in tennis. He'd discovered from taking the Tennis Mind-

Body Checklist that he was an E-A Need Type. He came to understand that his emotions caused him to lose attentional focus during those parts of a tennis match that he perceived as stressful.

This insight helped him see that he needed to keep a relatively steady and positive flow of emotions throughout the match. Over the past half year he'd learned how to control his attention and, perhaps more important, how to keep tennis in perspective so every possible situation in a match was viewed as an opportunity and not as a crisis.

His research into the mental aspects of tennis began in earnest as he learned that in any match there are different things to focus on depending on the task at hand. He'd become quite natural at shifting his attention from broad to narrow and back again as different parts of a match unfolded. Likewise, he developed an expertise at shifting his focus from internal thoughts and images to external cues and task-relevant stimuli.

To help keep things that had previously stressed him from affecting his generally good tennis technique, he learned about the power of imagery. He practiced it to calm himself down when he felt that he was being overly aroused by the stimulation of competition. He used personal imagery scripts to activate his energy system when he needed to be higher or lower in arousal.

Perhaps the best thing he learned was to overcome his fears in tennis. He had always felt strongly about embarrassing himself in front of others. He came to learn that fear kills confidence; and without confidence nothing in tennis, nor in any other endeavor, was possible.

Additionally, he learned about the importance of goal setting, and he set up a series of difficult yet reachable goals that would help him demonstrate excellent tennis technique during the festival's competition. One of the things that really gave him confidence going into the festival was the fact that he was now concentrating on the attainment of specific performance goals and not outcome goals. He felt energized knowing that if he concentrated on task-relevant cues and emphasized quality positioning, smart shot selection, mobility, and a good attitude, he had a personal yardstick for performance improvements that was much healthier and controllable than worrying about whether he won or lost.

As he began to make his first serve, he noted the strong wind in his face and immediately viewed it as a challenge worth a technique adjustment, not as a problem worth fretting over. This attitude about the wind gave him yet another dose of confidence—which in turn affected his posture and bearing. He noted that his confident self-image was not lost on his first opponent, who appeared to be overly energized. Just before delivering service, he felt an overpowering calmness because he knew that he was more focused on playing well than on the final score. He felt free, alive, and in the mood for an outstanding match, whatever the outcome. Although he knew that he was a relatively inexperienced tennis player, he knew that he had done everything he could to become a smart tennis player. He took a breath, tossed the ball, and began the best match of his career.

Ben's story is a great one, for he learned to squeeze the most out of his abilities by his using all the mind-body tools available. If you've been following along closely, you're probably excited about putting your new self-knowledge and mind-body skills to the test. You've discovered your greatest needs by completing the TMBC in Chapter One, and reviewed strategies to help you enjoy the game more and perform better.

Now it's time to put it all together and play smart tennis. It will work for you. During a major tournament, one of my students summed up her feelings about her comprehensive mental skills training program:

I am more excited about tennis than ever before, not only because I made it to the semifinals but because I have finally found the key to mental toughness. Sport psychology teaches you to ignore the distractions and concentrate instead on becoming the best you can be!

Because smart players are interested in, pay attention to, and learn about all of the most important aspects of their sport, we could conclude our smart tennis journey by touching upon a variety of factors that ultimately affect tennis performance. Such factors include equipment, physical training procedures (for strength, aerobic conditioning, flexibility, anaerobic power, and agility), nutrition, injury care and prevention, stroke biomechanics, and motor learning protocols. Covering all these and other important topics (sport physiology, body composition, and social issues, to name a few more) is really beyond the scope of this book. That said, however, I do feel that two of these factors do complement our trek toward smarter tennis strongly enough to merit attention here: nutrition and coping with injury. After these important factors are discussed, we'll conclude by integrating everything we've covered via practical pointers on what to do before, during, and after every match. Once you've applied this knowledge on the court, your opponents might ask what tennis academy you've been secretly attending. Smile and tell them you're just playing smarter!

> Of all the human powers operating on the affairs of mankind, none is greater than that of competition.
> —Henry Clay

The Mind-Body Domino Effect

Chapters Two through Six introduced you to attention control, imagery, confidence, energy control, and goal setting. You saw how these five mind-body skills influence your thoughts, emotions, actions, and physical sensations. These smart tennis tools always interact with one another to affect your performance. For example, just as positive imagery raises your confidence, effective attention control keeps you properly energized and goal focused. Mastery in one area boosts skills in other areas. Unfortunately the reverse is also true. A serious deficit in one area undercuts the others, and a real domino effect can come into play! For example, when your confidence is low, it's often hard to stay properly energized. Your ongoing challenge is to achieve excellence by balancing all five skills. This journey differs for every individual.

Some players thrive on high energy while others perform better remaining calm. Visual imagery works wonders for some, and others place greater emphasis on kinesthetic simulation. Although it takes practice and experience to achieve personal mind-body balance, it's worth your every effort. It's been said that ignorance is bliss, but self-ignorance usually impairs both performance and enjoyment, whether in tennis, golf, or board meetings!

Advancing to Less Effort

As your self-understanding increases and mind-body techniques improve, playing smart tennis becomes more natural. With the advanced attention control learned in

Chapter Two, for example, you're more fascinated in the moment and require less conscious effort or control. Your automatic pilot takes over and allows you to perform naturally. Your progress takes place in identifiable stages. First you evaluate your strengths and weaknesses to gain self-knowledge, next you learn and apply appropriate mind-body skills, and finally these skills become just another natural aspect of performance. At more advanced levels of play, for example, even fine adjustments made in the heat of battle have been worked out long in advance through imagery.

With competition fast approaching, let's first review some basic considerations regarding nutrition and injury coping.

Tennis Nutrition 101

Although we've already discussed mind-body fuels in Chapter Five, there's another form of energy that's even more basic to tennis and survival—food! Three types of food energy are carbohydrates, proteins, and fats. Each of these groups provides an important function to your body. There are as many recommendations for proper nutrition on the market as there are people, but an overall diet containing all three food types is definitely recommended.

Diets restricted to only one or two of these groups

cannot supply all the nutrients you need. Caloric intake is important as well—both overeating and undereating may pose significant health problems in addition to reducing your performance. I've seen lots of eating disorders (anorexia, bulimia, and so on) among athletes in various clinical and athletic settings. These problems are much more common than you might think. If you suspect that you or someone you know has an eating disorder, seek professional care as these problems often pose a serious threat to health.

Carbohydrates such as pasta, breads, fruit, and vegetables are metabolized quickly into blood sugar, providing an excellent source of energy. They are smart tennis foods, but too many carbohydrates can lead to a sugar crash and complete exhaustion. Fats provide a more long-term energy source and are found in many foods such as butter, cheese, meats, and oils. However, fats are much more difficult to digest than carbohydrates, and too much fat is harmful. Finally, proteins are most utilized by the body after carbohydrate and fat stores have been depleted. Proteins are found in foods such as meat, fish, eggs, and dairy products, and are important for tissue repair and growth.

Balance is the key to healthy nutrition. Both food quantity and quality should be closely regulated. Too many calories of any food, no matter how healthy, will be stored as fat. On the other end of the scale (no pun intended!) restrictive diets almost never work either. Generally seek to consume lower amounts of fat, moderate amounts of protein, and higher amounts of carbohydrates. Eat plenty of complex carbohydrates such as fruits and vegetables, and avoid the cheap sugars found in candy, pastries, and soft drinks. Also avoid fast foods. Drink plenty of water before, during, and after your match. Water is my favorite smart tennis beverage, but mixing in a small amount of fruit juice, or your favorite sport drink, also works. Make sure to stay well hydrated and take many small sips throughout the match rather than consuming large amounts of fluid in one sitting.

A light pre-game meal, two to three hours before the match, should consist of carbohydrates such as fruits, vegetables, and pasta. Continue drinking water up until match time. Proteins and fats are harder to digest and should be eaten in extremely small quantities, if at all, before competition. Dairy products, refined sugar, and alcohol should never be consumed prior to playing. Small pieces of fruit (such as bananas and oranges) make a great on-court snack. Following the match, take care not to overeat just to satisfy your temporary post-competition appetite.

Having reviewed some basic nutritional tips, let's take a look at another area that has a tremendous impact on your overall well being and match day performance—injuries.

Coping with Injuries

Injuries are inevitable in all sports, including tennis. They're such a great source of stress that some have called injuries the most important issue in sport. The trick is to learn how to cope effectively once they've occurred.

Mike Wasik—a certified athletic trainer and former tennis trainer (and head football trainer) for the University of Florida Athletic Association—told me that in his experience, the most common tennis injuries are tendinitis of the rotator cuff (shoulder) and tennis elbow. By contrast, golfers most frequently experience low back strains and hip pain, and runners find their most common injuries involve lower extremity problems such as shin splints and heel pain.

Injuries can lead to emotional problems, including anxiety and depression, and unhealthy behaviors such as increased drug and alcohol use. These negative moods and behaviors place the athlete at risk for prolonged rehabilitation and further behavioral problems.

Although there are an estimated seventeen million sport injuries in the United States annually, surprisingly little research has examined the consequences of sport injury or the psychological factors that promote healing. For example, why do some athletes adjust to injury with increased optimism and effort, while others—even with less severe physical damage—plunge into the depths of depression or fail to comply with treatment recommendations?

These questions prompted me to pursue this topic for my Ph.D. dissertation at the University of Florida. I examined how over seventy athletes (including tennis players) and over thirty football players from the 1996 national champion Florida Gators football team adjusted emotionally to injury. Although the majority adjusted well, many others reported moods including anger, depression, anxiety, confusion, fatigue, and reduced vigor.

Although more severe injuries obviously occur in contact sports such as football and boxing, injured tennis players also endure distress from a number of losses. These may include lost conditioning and match toughness, forfeited scholarships, lower self-esteem, or just the loss of a rewarding outlet. Clinical sport psychologists are becoming fully integrated members of the world's best sports medicine teams, involved in all aspects of athlete care including injury prevention, assessment, and rehabilitation. Whether you have access to this service or not, here are some tips to help you cope with a difficult injury. Keep in mind that these tips are never a substitute for qualified professional care:

- Maintain a positive yet realistic attitude about injury diagnosis and treatment options. Remain flexible. If your injury keeps you from hitting an

overhead, work on other skills (such as volleys or footwork) or on your overall conditioning.
- Examine what the injury means to you in terms of loss, and discuss your feelings openly with a friend. The sincere attention provided by others goes a long way toward recovery, and social support protects against stress.
- Successful performance imagery—as described in Chapter Three—should be used to keep your skills and strategies sharp and to help defeat the fear of repeated injury when regular practice is impossible.
- As you discovered in Chapter Six, challenging yet attainable short- and long-term goals should be set to monitor progress and speed recovery.

Now let's turn our attention back to more specific pre-match activities to help you manage competition effectively.

Before the Match

Many tennis players think that the match begins with the first serve. Technically this is correct, but realistically it's a serious blunder. Although the chair umpire rarely asks you what you had for breakfast or how you're coping with your nagging rotator cuff, these factors powerfully influence performance. In fact, everything you do from the day before your match until showtime influences your performance.

Elite performers in many situations adopt more consistent pre-performance activities than their less skilled counterparts. In my opinion, this applies to all sports, performing arts, and business. My wife, a professional ballerina selected by Mikhail Baryshnikov to attend the American Ballet Theatre's School of Classical Ballet, uses a regular pre-performance routine before going on stage. In a slightly less delicate situation, one 310-pound offensive lineman I know engages in consistent imagery while putting on his shoulder pads before kick-off. Many corporate executives prepare for important presentations by silently rehearsing key points of their speech. Whether in ballet, business, football, or tennis, pre-performance routines are powerful and necessary.

Keep a record of your routines by writing them down on a large index card. In the beginning, refer to your card throughout all the pre-performance stages. After a while, you won't need the card—but use it as long as necessary to refine your routines based on what works best. The following are some more smart tennis recommendations for the pre-match phase.

Pack Your Tennis Bag

In his 1993 book, *Winning Ugly,* tennis professional Brad Gilbert recommended the following items in his "equipment checklist" as the minimum to put together before a match: water, two rackets, energy food, Flex-All 454 (for sore muscles), ibuprofen, chemical ice, towels, sweatbands, cap with visor, dry shirts, and additional equipment as needed. I'd add to this list the following items: wristbands, extra grip tape, a folding chair, tissue paper, extra socks, extra shoes, notebook and pencil, *Smart Tennis,* and copies of your smart tennis goal sheets from Chapter Six. Pack these items the day before your match and you'll be ready the next morning with fewer hassles.

Before Sleeping

Sleep is important. Without proper sleep you'll be restless, agitated, and less focused on a winning performance. Avoid caffeine or large meals the evening before your match, and eat your dinner early in the evening. Review your five key mind-body skills and your goals for the following day. Reread the *Smart Tennis* tips at the end of each chapter if you just need a refresher. Before counting sheep, engage in a quality session of prophetic imagery for nine minutes, covering the before, during, and after aspects of performance for three minutes each. (See Chapter Three for a refresher on prophetic imagery.) Upon awakening, remind yourself of your goals, and again imagine a perfect performance.

Stretch Properly

Before you practice or play, it's important to engage in a stretching routine for several minutes. This helps prevent injury and provides flexibility for performance. Stretching also promotes healthy blood flow to transport nutrients throughout your system, and takes lactic acid out of fatigued muscles to reduce soreness. Although there are many ways to stretch, here are some basic guidelines to follow in developing and maintaining a good stretching routine before you even pick up your racket:

- Lightly warm up your core temperature by doing a slow jog or by lightly running in place. Slightly elevating your core temperature inhibits the *stretch reflex,* which prevents a full range of motion when your muscles are cold. Three or four laps around the court on a warm day—six or eight if the outside temperature is cold—should be sufficient to inhibit the stretch reflex.
- Once your core temperature is elevated slightly, stretch all your important muscles slowly and gradually in a static fashion. Never bounce up and down on your muscles as this may lead to injury.
- Employ a moderate stretch tension and hold it for several seconds. Always end the stretch

before you feel pain. Trust your body to tell you when enough is enough.

- After you've stretched out, jog in place or jump rope to induce a light sweat, if you haven't begun sweating already. Spend more time stretching on a cold day and make sure you're completely warm before finishing. Stay warm until your match begins!

Scouting Your Opponent's Mind-Body Skills

Pre-match scouting is smart. It allows you to prepare a plan specific to the challenge. You need to understand your opponent's technical skill level (the strokes and strategies you're likely to face), mind-body strengths and weaknesses, and physical fitness level. Many players know how to exploit their opponent's poor technique and fitness, but you want to use our opponent's mind-body shortcomings to your advantage.

Let's begin studying your opponent's abilities in each of the five mind-body areas, with strategies on how to exploit mind-body weaknesses.

Poor Attention Control

Study the player's eyes. Does he or she easily lose concentration when confronted with noises or sights outside the playing area? Easily get distracted by a particular style of play (such as net approaches)? Players with poor attention control are the easiest to exploit. Plan on mixing in lots of different shots (for example, topspin, backspin), varying the pace and placements of your shots, and employing a variety of different strategies (say, first serve and volley, then stay back). Play extremely consistent tennis. The combination of long rallies and unpredictable play will drive these players crazy! You'll pull an occasional upset just by exploiting poor attention control.

Poor Imagery

How could you possibly know if your opponent is using proper imagery during a match? You really can't, but good predictions are possible. If the player rushes between points, takes varying amounts of time before serving, or fails to spend quiet time alone between points and games, there's a good chance you've detected someone who doesn't use regular imagery. No matter how great people who fail to use imagery may appear, they're not as well prepared as they could be. This makes them susceptible to mental errors. Have patience when such an opponent plays well, because it won't last long. Keep the ball in play and surprise the opponent every once in a while with unconventional play. For example, hit the ball down the line when you would normally hit crosscourt, or serve and volley on your second serve. Exploit this player's lack of preparation by playing steady, but go against the norm more than usual.

Confidence Problems

Look for signs of low confidence such as dejection, sluggish movements, or verbal self-abuse. When you suspect that your next opponent lacks confidence on the court, make sure to do nothing to change that useful self-image. Start out strong to establish your dominance. When you play first points well, you feed your opponent's self-doubts. Present a confident image throughout the match. Even when you're behind in score, realize that just a slight momentum swing in your favor will raise more self-doubt in your opponent's mind.

On the other hand, when you suspect your next opponent is overconfident, allow the delusion to continue by remaining quiet and appearing humble (while keeping the fire burning inside!). Overconfident players are easy to topple since they usually lack effort and consistency. Capitalize on your opportunities when their effort wavers. Since these players never perform up to their potential, there is every possibility of an upset victory.

Energy Problems

Assess the energy levels of your upcoming opponent. Do you see signs of overexcitement or apathy? If so, your goal is to make sure that these energy levels remain the same—or even go further off-kilter—during the match. Speed up the pace of play against an opponent who appears high-strung or anxious. You can accomplish this in many ways—rushing the net more, taking your time before serves (within the time allotted), or taking shorter breaks between games. As we learned in Chapter Five, an opponent whose energy levels are too high will miss important cues, so give them as much to think about in as short a time as possible. Vary your style of play, shot selection, and pace. After hitting a topspin floater and rushing the net, you may be able to slip in an advance unnoticed! The narrow focus makes it hard for your opponent to react to variety.

> There's nobody out there who has perfect stuff. The idea is to win with what you've got.
> —John McEnroe

On the other hand, when your opponent appears overly relaxed, slow down and allow as many natural distractions as possible to take their toll. Appear calm and passive, but stay mentally alert to quickly capitalize on their low energy. Lull them to sleep and only wake them up again after the match is over!

Poor Goals

Players without effective goals are easy to manipulate. They might play a lot but they still don't know what they want to accomplish. They might dwell on outcomes rather than focusing on performance, and their play lacks purpose. Many also whine about the score or overreact following important points. The first key to exploiting this weakness is to realize that you're the boss. People with poor direction and focus will often react to your moves rather than developing creative strategies of their own. Stay centered on your own performance. If their shots are inconsistent too, allow them to make errors. If they have no weapons but just bring every ball back, plan on moving them around, varying the pace, and taking them out of their comfort zone by forcing them to make shots they don't enjoy.

Before we move on to match considerations, it's important to note that you will eventually meet other smart tennis players. Know what they are looking for in your play and mannerisms!

During the Match

Let's turn our attention to the actual match. You've prepared well and scouted your opponent's tendencies. Now it's time to turn on your automatic pilot and play smart tennis. Here are some strategies while out on the court.

- *Point routines.* The point is the most basic unit in tennis. Play each point well and you'll have a great match. As you walk up to the service line or adjust your position to return serve, it's important to be totally prepared. Quiet your mind, recall your specific goal for the point, and then imagine it to perfection with confidence. Visualize a sequence of at least three shots. Modify your energy levels, if needed, and narrow your focus to the task at hand.

It's important to be natural and let your instincts take over once the point begins. This is the essence of smart tennis. Enjoy the challenge of expressing your physical and mental strengths to the best of your ability.

Once the point is over, make a quick note of what just happened. Perhaps the opponent just passed you down the line. Perhaps your kick serve to the opponent's backhand forced a weak return. Store these facts away for future reference. Also take note of strategy, strengths, and weaknesses. You'll be surprised at how well your memory serves your future decisions. Prepare any changes for the next point, return to the pre-point stage, and repeat the cycle.

- *Changeover routine.* After the first game, have a seat, sip water, and totally relax. Many players sit with a towel over their heads to stay focused and reduce external distractions.

Quickly assess what worked and didn't work last game by reviewing the notes you've mentally made to yourself following the points. Do you see any trends? Are you accomplishing your goals? What happened that you didn't anticipate? Don't dwell on negatives. Just relax, observe, and begin making mental notes for the next game.

Review your main goals for the next game and imagine a point to perfection that will take you there. Set your energy levels, confidence, and attention, and go back out to the court with a renewed sense of purpose and challenge.

- *Change strategy slowly.* Throughout a match it's easy to want to change things quickly when the going gets rough. Resist these impulses and stay with the basics. For example, you might have determined that your opponent's backhand is a weakness—but at the net it still got past you twice in a row! Don't trash your plan too soon. Keep your strategy until your opponent has convinced you that your plan was faulty from the outset. After the first set, reevaluate where you've been and where you're going. This is a great time to make a major shift in strategy if it's necessary.
- *Momentum management.* Momentum is another element to consider in any competitive situation. In tennis, shifts in momentum are notorious. I can't remember the number of matches I've seen where momentum shifts stole the show. For example, you might win the first eight games, and take a 6–0, 2–0 advantage, before the momentum shifts and your opponent reels off eight games against you. Now the score is 6–0, 2–6, 0–2! What a potentially threatening experience. For the inexperienced, it's like winning the lottery and then losing your ticket on the way to collect! Smart tennis players expect momentum to change at any time,

because it does. When the pendulum swings back in your favor, you might win the next six games in a row for a 6–0, 2–6, 6–2 win.

• *Managing mind games.* It's often said that all's fair in love and war. What about tennis? What are the limits of acceptable behavior in this game shrouded by noble traditions? In my opinion, there's a fine line between tactical gamesmanship and crude dishonesty or cheating. Cheating is reprehensible and should never be encouraged or tolerated. What about subtle ways of seizing the competitive advantage—verbal threats, cold stares, or other methods of distracting the opponent? Should gamesmanship be trained to perfection like a finely crafted backhand, or discouraged and criticized as unsportsmanlike? Were John McEnroe's timely outbursts acceptable—or a disgrace to his character and the game? It's surprising that so few experts have studied these issues.

Well-developed mental skills (staying focused, optimally energized, and performance oriented) help us excel in a variety of performance situations, including tennis. However, just as these psychological tools enhance performance, there are quite a few clever anti-tools available to nullify the positive effects of mind-body skills! A wily foe might do everything in his or her power to destroy your confidence and break your concentration. The bottom line is that if you want to be your very best, don't assume that everyone will give you the respect you deserve. Make an effort to study the nasty antics of the bad people too.

The following are three examples of mind games in action and how to react when your opponent tries them. I'm sure you can think of more.

- *Purposely forgetting the score.* This is done to throw off your attention and make you doubt yourself. Ask politely that your opponent repeat the score clearly after every point. If this doesn't work, volunteer to do it yourself.
- *Complimenting your "amazing shot."* By throwing the spotlight on the genius of your last shot, your opponent cleverly distracts you by having you overanalyze your strokes. This undermines your confidence as it would be "impossible to do that again!" After these kinds of compliments, say thank you or nothing at all, then just smile to yourself and say "nice try."
- *Challenging your eyesight.* Players at all levels will go out of their way to challenge your line calls. This may range from a silent stare to a verbal barrage. The purpose is always to get you to question your judgment and throw off your rhythm. Play fairly and always give the benefit of any doubt to your opponent, but don't undermine your own judgment and confidence.

Although fairness and sportsmanship are values in sport, many disregard these virtues to their own disadvantage. One top junior tennis player I worked with won his match and reported the score, only to realize that his opponent had already reported a fabricated outcome to the tournament director! Since there were no outside witnesses, the match had to be replayed. This kind of competition ruins the sport for everyone. Luckily it's the exception rather than the rule.

There will probably never be a universal consensus regarding what constitutes fair play. In an ideal world, tennis would only be a fun endeavor promoting fitness, skill development, and a healthy test of physical and mental strength. Unfortunately, competitive situations often bring out a more devious and self-serving beast.

Luckily, a player's reputation spreads far and wide. Once players become known as poor sports, their ability to harm others with their antics is greatly reduced. Work hard to keep your mind-body skills in top condition, while anticipating some of the mind games that might be used against you.

After the Match

The first thing to do following any match is to greet your opponent with a smile and say thank you for the experience. The following are a number of slightly more formal steps to follow as a smart tennis player.

- *Debriefing imagery.* Go back to Chapter Three and perform debriefing imagery. This helps you reinforce good habits and extinguish bad ones.

• *Review your goals and behavior.* Take out your daily goal worksheet from Chapter Six and evaluate your performance. On a scale of 1 to 10, rate how closely you came to achieving each of your daily goals. If you're always receiving 10s, you'll need to set your goals higher next time. On the other hand, 1s mean that you're shooting for the stars, and possibly in a state of delusion!

Also review each of the specific behaviors you chose to accomplish in your daily goals and rate these on the same 1–10 scale. Do you see any patterns in your ratings? Have you chosen behaviors that lead to performance accomplishments? By completing this brief procedure after every competition, you'll gradually become an expert goal setter and achiever, and recognize patterns in your behavior that you never knew existed.

Explaining Match Outcome

Following every match there's a winner—and a player who didn't win. Notice that I didn't use the term *loser* because we all win in this great sport! How you explain the match outcome to yourself often influences your emotional reactions to the outcome and the level of motivation you'll bring to your next performance. Here are some brief tips on how to explain your match outcomes to yourself and remain positive and motivated at the same time.

- *Following a loss.* Tell yourself to try harder the next time in achieving your performance goals. Never attribute your loss to low ability. Remember that you ultimately control only how well you perform. You might have just played the best match of your life but lost because the other player's name was Davenport or Rafter!
- *Following a win.* Give yourself a pat on the back and attribute your victory to both high effort and ability. Don't explain away your efforts as just luck or an easy opponent. The fact is that you achieved success, and credit is due.
- *Start and finish with the positives.* Many players I've worked with easily recalled a million things that went wrong after their matches, whether they won or lost. Since they're so achievement oriented, they're often quicker to recognize flaws, but may also miss many positives. Whatever your level of play, keep a balanced perspective. Don't go too far in either direction. You'll recall many things you did well and many things you could have done better. In any self-evaluation, begin with positives and end with positives. Somewhere in between, review what you'd like to do better next time.

Take Stock of Your Mind-Body Skills

Before you go to bed on the evening after your match, go over the five mind-body skills again to see which areas posed difficulties and which areas showed improvement. If you balance these subtleties often, you'll find the path to a higher level of play. For example, you might notice that your confidence rose and fell throughout the match, and that your greatest problems were in expressing confidence. With this in mind, you can set firm goals next match to portray an extremely positive body image.

Frequently review the chapters in this book. The skills that you have acquired to become a smart tennis player can be practiced and refined just as often as your physical skills. It's amazing how easy it is to forget to apply mind-body principles even though you might know them well. There's no magic pill or mantra that will align your mental and physical skills in a perfect state of harmony, so you'll have to rely on your own efforts, intuition, and personal judgment to keep getting better.

The Higher Road to Growth and Confidence

In this fast-paced world of athletic achievement and endless pursuits it's often overlooked that tennis is just a sport. As a sport, tennis should neither threaten self-esteem nor evoke hostility. At least these are the ideals! Tennis should be fun, challenging, and fulfilling, even at the professional level. Unfortunately many players lose sight of this truth and turn a potentially rewarding activity into a game of Russian roulette, awaiting destruction from self-imposed pressure and fear.

Sport has often been called a metaphor for life, simulating the ups and downs, positives and negatives, courage and fear. By competing regularly, we expose our weaknesses and stretch our mind-body capacities to the limit. For the smart tennis player, this is greatly satisfying, for challenges make us stronger and force us to adapt better in the future. What is really great is that the benefits of playing tennis can also spill over into real life.

Outcomes in tennis are only determined by what happens during the match—so it's pointless to obsess over the final score. Although the match result is one measure of progress, it's vastly overrated. Since our society glorifies success, the first question often heard following a match is, "Did you win or lose?" What a dull and abrupt inquiry! What about the fun, the challenge, the growth, the experience?

Don't misread me. Some might like to eliminate the score and change the rules so that the player who experiences the most interpersonal growth receives the trophy. This would eliminate my interest in tennis immediately! I might even dust off my golf clubs! Competition is natural and healthy and we should strive vigorously to win; but the important word is *strive*. Once the match is won, there are hundreds more to play and our thirst is never really quenched. Although winning is an obvious objective, it's really just a label for all the activity preceding it. Consciously focusing on winning actually impairs performance. By tuning into excellence and personal growth, both on and off the court, you'll rid yourself of the fear of failure and allow yourself to focus on being the best you can be. Confidence will prosper, and so will you.

Let's finish up by looking at some areas where regular competitive tennis can lead to personal growth, satisfaction, and confidence:

- *Problem solving enhancement.* Problems on the court begin to be viewed as exciting puzzles rather than threatening sources of future failure.
- *Renewal of energies.* A good heated battle distracts you from the more serious problems in life, renews your batteries, and increases your level of fitness.
- *Adversity off the court.* Dealing with difficulty on the court may help boost your confidence in dealing with real-life problems too.
- *Self-esteem enhancement.* When self-esteem is measured by factors under your control (such as trying hard or defeating the inner fears) rather than outcome (winning or losing), you're no longer at risk for self-depreciation following a loss.

I really hope you've enjoyed your journey toward becoming a smart tennis player. It's been a pleasure guiding you in this pursuit. Have a great time as your game continues to improve!

References

Ahsen, A. (1972). *Eidetic Parents Test and Analysis.* New York: Brandon House.

Ahsen, A. (1984). ISM: The triple code model for imagery and psychophysiology. *Journal of Mental Imagery,* 8, 15–42.

Connors, J. (1986). *How to play tougher tennis.* New York: Golf Digest/Tennis.

Cox, R. H. (1990). *Sport psychology: Concepts and applications.* Dubuque, IA: W. C. Brown.

Gilbert, B., & Jamison, S. (1993). *Winning ugly.* New York: Fireside.

Hanin, Y. L. (1986). A study of anxiety in sports. In W. F. Straub (Ed.), *Sport psychology: An analysis of athlete behavior.* Ithaca, NY: Mouvement.

Hardy, L. (1990). A catastrophe model of performance in sport. In J. G. Jones & L. Hardy (Eds.), *Stress and performance in sport.* Chichester, England: Wiley.

Jacobson, E. (1929). *Progressive relaxation.* Chicago: University of Chicago Press.

Kerr, J. H. (1985). The experience of arousal: A new basis for studying arousal effects in sport. *Journal of Sport Sciences, 3,* 169–179.

Lang, P. J. (1979). A bio-informational theory of emotional imagery. *Psychophysiology, 17,* 495–512

Liebman, G. (1997). *Tennis shorts: 1,001 of the game's funniest one-liners.* Chicago: Contemporary Books.

Martens, R. (1987). *Coaches guide to sport psychology.* Champaign, IL: Human Kinetics.

McClelland, D. C., Atkinson, J. W., Clark, R. A., & Lowell, E. L. (1953). *The achievement motive.* Englewood Cliffs, NJ: Appleton-Century-Crofts.

Murray, J. F. (1998). *Emotional adjustment to sport injury: Effects of injury severity, social support, and athletic identity.* Dissertation Abstracts International.

Murray, J. F. (1998). Emotional adjustment to sport injury in elite and recreational athletes. Paper presented at the 1998 American Psychological Association meeting, San Francisco, CA.

Nideffer, R. (1981). *The ethics and practice of applied sport psychology.* Ithaca, NY: Mouvement.

Oxendine, J. B. (1984). *Psychology of motor learning.* Upper Saddle River, NJ: Prentice Hall.

Phillips, B. (1993). *Phillips' book of great thoughts and funny sayings.* Wheaton, IL: Tyndale House.

Sackett, R. S. (1934). The influences of symbolic rehearsal upon the retention of a maze habit. *Journal of General Psychology, 13,* 113–128.

Wallace, D. F. (1997). *A supposedly fun thing I'll never do again.* New York: Little, Brown.

White, A., & Hardy, L. (1995). Use of different imagery perspectives on learning and performance of different motor skills. *British Journal of Psychology, 86,* 169–180.

Recommended Reading

Braden, V., & Bruns, B. (1998). *Tennis 2000: Strokes, strategy, and psychology for a lifetime.* New York: Little, Brown.

Collins, B. (1997). *Bud Collins' tennis encyclopedia.* New York: Visible Ink Press.

Gallwey, W. T. (1997). *The inner game of tennis.* (Rev. ed.). New York: Random House.

Gilbert, B., & Jamison, S. (1993). *Winning ugly.* New York: Fireside.

Van Raalte, J. L., & Brewer, B. W. (Eds.). (1996). *Exploring sport and exercise psychology.* Washington, DC: American Psychological Association.

Weinberg, R. S., & Gould, D. (1995). *Foundations of sport and exercise psychology.* Champaign, IL: Human Kinetics.

About the Author

John F. Murray has an extensive background in playing and coaching tennis, writing and lecturing on sport psychology and tennis, and providing psychological services. After graduating from Loyola University in New Orleans, John obtained certification as a tennis professional through the United States Professional Tennis Association and United States Professional Tennis Registry. He then contracted to teach tennis in Munich, Germany. Subsequently, he taught tennis in Hawaii, Europe, North America, and the Middle East with Peter Burwash International tennis specialists. He coached five seasons at *Tennis Magazine*'s #1 rated tennis resort, Bio-Hotel Stanglwirt, in the Austrian Alps near Kitzbühel.

He also conducted mental training workshops, held a regular newspaper tennis column, and promoted tennis via radio. He later taught undergraduate tennis courses at the University of Florida, provided sport psychology workshops for the United States Tennis Association at the ATP Tour International Headquarters, and provided sport psychology consultation to the NCAA Division I tennis teams at Washington State University and Florida International University.

He completed his graduate studies at the University of Florida, where he received master's degrees both in exercise and sport sciences and in clinical psychology, and a Ph.D. in clinical psychology in 1998. His doctoral dissertation focused on the national champion Florida Gators football team. As a clinical psychology intern, he also completed a full-year rotation in applied sport psychology through the Department of Intercollegiate Athletics at Washington State University. John is currently on the faculty of the Counseling and Psychological Services Center at Florida International University.

He contributes to the psychology of tennis in his award-winning sport psychology column, "Mental Equipment." John continues to enjoy playing tennis and recently received a #16 end-of-year ranking in the Men's Open Singles Division of the Florida Section of the United States Tennis Association.

He is a member of Division 47 (Exercise and Sport Sciences) of the American Psychological Association, and of the Association for the Advancement of Applied Sport Psychology. Dr. Murray's web page is located at http://www.SmartTennis.com and e-mails to him can be directed to DrJohn@SmartTennis.com.

About the General Editor

Rick Frey has an impressive record in the physical activity field. A former professor of kinesiology at San Diego State University (SDSU) in the 1970s, he was a racquetball teaching professional, weight-loss coordinator, and health fitness leader at the prestigious Canyon Racquet Club in Salt Lake City, Utah, during the early 1980s, professor and chairperson of the department of physical education at the University of Alaska, Anchorage (UAA), between 1982 and 1988, and director of the academic book division of Human Kinetics Publishers in Champaign, Illinois, between 1988 and 1996.

A thirty-year rugby veteran, he coached the sport at both the University of Alberta (UA) in Edmonton, Canada, and the University of Illinois (UI). He also coached wrestling (UA) and ice hockey (UAA) and served as the sport psychology consultant to numerous individual and team sport athletes at UAA, SDSU, and

UI for more than a dozen years. Athletes he has consulted with have gone on to earn All-American, professional, and Olympic honors.

Former president of the Alaska Association for Health, Physical Education, Recreation, and Dance, Frey has written more than thirty professional and scholarly articles and a book chapter and has given papers at more than fifty state, regional, and national conferences in the physical activity field.

With graduate degrees in sport psychology and human motor performance, he is currently an adjunct professor of kinesiology and outdoor recreation at the Eastern Sierra College Center of Cerro Coso Community College in Bishop, California, where he also serves as a senior exercise specialist to more than 120 older adults for the Inyo County Office of Education. He is currently vice president of acquisitions and development at Exercise Science Publishing, Inc., a division of Sagamore Publishing.

Index

D

E

This page constitutes a continuation of the copyright page.

The quote in Chapter One by David Foster Wallace from *A Supposedly Fun Thing I'll Never Do Again* is reprinted by permission of Little, Brown and Company.

Exhibit 1.1, "The Tennis Mind-Body Checklist," is reprinted by permission of the author. Copyright © 1996 by John F. Murray. All rights reserved.

Exhibit 2.1, "Examples of Combinations of Attentional Focus in Tennis," from *The Ethics and Practice of Applied Sport Psychology* by Robert M. Nideffer is reprinted by permission of Mouvement Publications.

Figure 2.3, "The Effects of Stress on Attention," is reprinted by permission from *Coaches Guide to Sport Psychology* by R. Martens. Champaign, Ill: Human Kinetics, 1987, p. 145.

Exhibit 4.1, "The National Tennis Rating Program," is reprinted by permission of the United States Tennis Association.

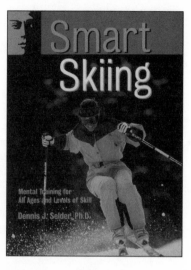